CW01238850

James: Jewish Roots, Catholic Fruits

James
Jewish Roots, Catholic Fruits

SHANE KAPLER

Angelico Press

First published in the USA
by Angelico Press 2021
Copyright © Shane Kapler 2021
All rights reserved:
No part of this book may be reproduced or transmitted,
in any form or by any means, without permission

Angelico Press, Ltd.
169 Monitor St., Brooklyn, NY 11222
www.angelicopress.com

978-1-62138-690-2 pb
978-1-62138-691-9 cloth
978-1-62138-692-6 ebook

Book and cover design
by Michael Schrauzer
Cover image: James Tissot (1836–1902). *Saint James the Less* (*Saint Jacques le Mineur*), 1886–1894.

NIHIL OBSTAT: Reverend John P. Cush, STD,
Censor Librorum of the Diocese of Brooklyn

IMPRIMATUR: Most Reverend
Nicholas DiMarzio, Ph.D., D.D.
Bishop of Brooklyn
Brooklyn, New York, December 23, 2020

Unless otherwise stated, the Scripture citations used in this work are taken from the *Second Catholic Edition of the Revised Standard Version of the Bible* (RSV), copyright © 1965, 1966, and 2006 by the Division of Christian Education of the National Council of the Churches of Christ in the United States of America. Used with permission. All rights reserved.

Scripture quotations marked (NABRE) are taken from the *New American Bible, Revised Edition* © 2010, 1991, 1986, 1970 Confraternity of Christian Doctrine, Washington, D.C. and are used by permission of the copyright owner. All Rights Reserved. No part of the New American Bible may be reproduced in any form without permission in writing from the copyright owner.

Scripture quotations marked (NIV) are taken from the *Holy Bible, New International Version*®, NIV®. Copyright © 1973, 1978, 1984, 2011 by Biblica, Inc.™ Used by permission of Zondervan. All rights reserved worldwide. www.zondervan.com. The "NIV" and "New International Version" are trademarks registered in the United States Patent and Trademark Office by Biblica, Inc.™

Excerpts from the English translation of the *Catechism of the Catholic Church* for use in the United States of America copyright © 1994, United States Catholic Conference, Inc.—Libreria Editrice Vaticana. Used with Permission.

For
Kevin Vost,
who *literally* wrote the book on friendship;
I am forever in your debt.

CONTENTS

ACKNOWLEDGMENTS x
INTRODUCTION 1

1 The Epistle's Inclusion in the New Testament 3
2 Our Author and the Family of Jesus 17
3 Salvation—A Synergy of Faith and Works 31
4 The Redemptive Nature of Suffering 53
5 Sacred Tradition, Source of the Written Gospels 71
6 Social Justice: The Gospel's Economic Demands 87
7 Anointing and Prayer: Healing for Body and Soul 103

CONCLUSION 127
BIBLIOGRAPHY 129

ACKNOWLEDGMENTS

MY SINCERE THANKS TO TONI ACETO, WHOSE interest in my work on Hebrews was a great impetus for undertaking this study of James, and Kevin Vost, who not only strongly encouraged me to undertake this project but postponed his own writing on James while I did so. I am also deeply grateful to Tony Grossman, Thomas Storck, Jill Deardorff, and Matt Nelson for reading and offering their invaluable feedback on individual chapters—and especially Michael Vento and Phillip Kapler for their profound insights and editorial comments on the entire manuscript. This is a far richer work because of them. Finally, I must thank my pastor, Fr. Michael Murphy, for preaching God's truth, no matter the season, and for sharing his experiences and insights from anointing the sick.

INTRODUCTION

> "Count it all joy, my brethren, when you meet various trials..."
>
> James 1:2

*W*HO BEGINS A SERMON THAT WAY? I know that I wouldn't; and I would be shocked to turn on my television and hear it from one of the purveyors of America's prosperity gospel. No, the only person I can imagine beginning an address with such a statement is Mother Teresa... or Francis of Assisi... or *Jesus*. Such counsel flies in the face of the therapeutic deism that masquerades as Christianity throughout so much of the West. It speaks to me of not just the cross, but the *crucifix*; and among Western Christians that is distinctively Catholic. In truth, James's entire epistle feels very "Catholic" to me—from its opening salvo right through to the final verses speaking of how salvation can be lost and regained.[1] James gives no quarter to the Christian who naively hopes that "once saved" means "always saved." Rather, James preaches the astounding truth entrusted by Christ to the apostles: that God's grace, freely communicated to us in the gifts of faith and baptism, requires a lifetime of our cooperation if it is to bring us to the fullness of life in heaven. Salvation is not a transaction but a *relationship* with the all-holy God.

Now, it is not just the Epistle of James that appears very "Catholic" to me, but the entire New Testament. In 2016, I wrote *The Epistle to the Hebrews and the Seven Core Beliefs of Catholics* in the conviction that, when that epistle is read with its original Jewish Christian audience in mind, it yields strikingly Catholic treasures. The same is demonstrably true of James and thus the book you are holding.[2]

---

[1] "My brethren, if any one among you wanders from the truth and some one brings him back, let him know that whoever brings back a sinner from the error of his way will save his soul from death and will cover a multitude of sins" (Jas 5:19–20).
[2] James's epistle is addressed to "the twelve tribes [of Israel] in the Dispersion" (1:1), indicating the need to place ourselves, as much as possible, into the sandals of James's first-century, Jewish Christian readers if we are to interpret him correctly.

James was a first-century Jew, well-versed in Hebrew Scripture and Greek culture, who came to believe that his kinsman, Jesus, was Israel's long-awaited Messiah. Unlike Judaism's high priest and the majority of its religious leaders, James understood that the New Covenant announced by Christ was not the repudiation of the Law and Temple but their fulfillment (Mt 5:17).

Jesus likened his Kingdom to a tiny seed that, under the Father's watchful eye, would grow into a vast tree in which the birds of the air would build their nests (Mt 13:31–32). In this book we will follow James's lead to see how the seed of revelation made to Abraham sprouted roots and grew throughout the time of Moses and the prophets until, watered by Christ's blood, it put forth the soaring, fruit-laden branches of Catholic life and doctrine in which all the men and women of the world are invited to dwell. We will fix our gaze upon five elements of Catholic belief: the necessity of both faith and works in obtaining final salvation, the redemptive nature of suffering, social justice, Sacred Tradition, and the efficacy of the Church's prayer and sacrament of healing. Each of these can be glimpsed in James's first chapter and are further developed by the author in the course of his letter. Instead of a verse-by-verse commentary, we will proceed thematically—tracing each theme through the text, looking at its history in Judaism and the way it is understood and lived in the Church today.[3]

Preliminary to this, however, we will spend time familiarizing ourselves with the history of the Epistle of James and its author. Not only will such knowledge provide a foundation for our study, but it will also impart important truths about the nature of Scripture and the earthly life of Jesus and his family—his mother in particular.

---

[3] In the course of our study, all but a handful of James's 108 verses will be considered.

CHAPTER 1

The Epistle's Inclusion in the New Testament

FOR TWENTY-FIRST-CENTURY CHRISTIANS the Epistle of James's status as an inspired work is a given, but that was not always the case. In this first chapter we will explore James's gradual acceptance by the Church at large, the doubts that reemerged at the time of the Reformation, and the theological conclusions to which such a history should lead us regarding the relationship between the Bible and the Church.

IN THE BEGINNING

The Epistle of James was composed sometime in the mid-first century. Once we settle on the identity of "James" we will be able to narrow the date of composition further. As I stated earlier, and will develop further in the next chapter, I identify the author as James, the bishop of Jerusalem and "brother" of Jesus, martyred in AD 62. For the purpose of this chapter, however, the author's exact identity is not decisive for dating the text to the mid-first century.

I say this because the Epistle of James was already available to Clement of Rome when he penned his *Epistle to the Corinthians*, c. AD 95. James is one of the New Testament's "catholic" epistles, meaning that it was not addressed to a specific congregation but to the Church universal.[1] We must, therefore, allow some period of time to have elapsed between the epistle's writing, its arrival in Rome, and Clement's ability to familiarize himself enough with its content to incorporate it into his own thought. When Clement penned his epistle, the writings that came to make up the New Testament were rarely cited by name. When we consult the original Greek texts, however, Clement's dependence upon James becomes obvious. Consider the following example:[2]

---

[1] The other "catholic" epistles are Jude, the two epistles of Peter, and the three of John.
[2] Luke Timothy Johnson, *Brother of Jesus, Friend of God: Studies in the Letter of James* (Grand Rapids, MI: Eerdmans, 2004), 55.

CHAPTER 30	EPISTLE OF JAMES
Seeing, therefore, that we are the portion of the Holy One, let us do all those things which pertain to holiness, avoiding all *evil-speaking* (*katalalia*), all abominable and impure embraces, together with all drunkenness, seeking after change, all *abominable lusts* (*epithymia*), detestable *adultery* (*moichia*), and execrable pride. *"For God,"* says [the Scripture], *"resists the proud, but gives grace to the humble* [Prov 3:34]*"* Let us cleave, then, to *those to whom grace has been given by God*. Let us clothe ourselves with concord and humility, ever exercising self-control, standing far off from all whispering and evil-speaking, *being justified by our works, and not our words*. For [the Scripture] says, "He that speaks much, shall also hear much in answer. *And does he that is ready in speech deem himself righteous?* Blessed is he that is born of woman, who lives but a short time: be not given to much speaking." Let our praise be in God, and not of ourselves; for God hates those *who commend themselves*. Let testimony to our good deeds be borne by others, as it was in the case of our righteous forefathers. Boldness, and arrogance, and audacity belong to those that are accursed of God; but *moderation (epieikeia), humility (tapeinophrosynē), and meekness (prautēs) to such as are blessed by Him*.³	*Draw near to God and he will draw near to you. Cleanse your hands*, you sinners, and purify your hearts.... (James 4:7–8) Do not *speak evil* (*katalaleite*) against one another (James 4:11) You desire (*epithymeite*) and do not have; so you kill. (James 4:2) Unfaithful creatures (*moichalides*)! (James 4:4) But *he gives more grace*; therefore it says, "God opposes the proud, but gives grace to the humble [Prov 3:34]." (Jas 4:6) *You see that a man is justified by works and not* by faith alone. (Jas 2:24) *If any one thinks he is religious, and does not bridle his tongue but deceives his heart*, this man's religion is vain. (Jas 1:26) As it is, *you boast in your arrogance. All such boasting is evil*. (Jas 4:16) But the wisdom from above is first pure, then peaceable, gentle (*epieikēs*), open to reason, full of mercy and good fruits, without uncertainty or insincerity. (Jas 3:17) Humble (*tapeinōthēte*) yourselves before the Lord and he will exalt you. (Jas 4:10) ... let him show his works in the meekness (*prautēti*) of wisdom. (Jas 3:13)

---

3 Clement of Rome, Letter to the Corinthians, https://www.ewtn.com/catholicism/library/first-epistle-to-the-corinthians-12498.

Other parallels can be noted, but the above is enough to establish the Epistle of James's existence and its use by a recognized shepherd of the Church prior to the end of the first century.

The fact that it was Clement of Rome who provides this first witness is significant. Clement was, after all, the third bishop of Rome in succession from Peter. His letter to the Church in Corinth, chastising its members for their rebellion against the ordained presbyters, demonstrates his authority within the larger Church. Clement ordered the Corinthians, "Accept our counsel and you will have nothing to regret.... If anyone disobeys the things which have been said by Him through us, let them know that they will involve themselves in transgression and in no small danger."[4] The Corinthians, rather than balk at the demands of a bishop some eight hundred miles away, repented. Eighty years later the bishop of Corinth wrote to Rome, telling Clement's successor how the letter was still read when the Church gathered on the Lord's Day.[5] That Clement drew from James in his admonition to the Corinthians is a testimony to James's wisdom and authority.

The second historical witness to James's usage is in *The Shepherd of Hermas*. The work's author, Hermas, was the brother of Pius I, Bishop of Rome from c. 140–154. *The Shepherd* is clearly dependent upon James, with thirty percent of James's text paralleled in the later work.[6] This dependence is most notable in *The Shepherd*'s first and third sections. Hermas's use of the word *dipsychos* (double-minded) is especially telling, since James is the only document in all of Greek literature to use it. James may well have coined the term (1:8, 4:8).[7]

THE BIBLICAL CANON BEGINS TO TAKE SHAPE

While we have evidence of James's early existence and usage, there was no push within the early Church to establish a canon, an authoritative list regarding which books should be recognized as "Christian" Scripture. That process did not begin until the latter

---

4 William A. Jurgens, *The Faith of the Early Fathers*, vol. 1 (Collegeville, MN: The Liturgical Press, 1970), 11.
5 Dionysius, *Letter to the Romans*, Fragment 2; preserved in Eusebius, *Ecclesiastical History* 4, 23.
6 Johnson, *Brother of Jesus*, 60.
7 Patrick J. Hartin, *James*, Sacra Pagina Series (Collegeville, MN: Liturgical Press, 2009), 7.

half of the second century. Many readers are probably unaware that Judaism also lacked a fixed canon at that point in time. In the first century the Sadducees appear to have recognized only the Torah—Genesis, Exodus, Leviticus, Numbers, and Deuteronomy—while the Pharisees recognized a group of texts corresponding closely, if not exactly, to today's Hebrew Scriptures. The Essenes, on the other hand, used a larger group of texts that contained the deuterocanonicals Sirach and Tobit as well as works later rejected by Judaism and Christianity such as Jubilees and 1 Enoch. Greek-speaking Jews, both inside and outside of the Holy Land, made use of a translation tradition known as the Septuagint that contained the works recognized by the Pharisees as well as the deuterocanonicals Tobit, Judith, Wisdom, Sirach, Baruch, 1 & 2 Maccabees, an additional 107 verses in the Book of Esther, and two chapters in the book of Daniel.[8] The Septuagint was the Scripture of the early Church. When the writers of the New Testament quoted the Old, eighty percent of the time they used the Septuagint. (The canon used by today's Judaism, which omits these works, was not settled until much later.)[9]

Before the end of the first century Jewish Christians had already begun to speak of the writings of the apostles and their close collaborators as "scripture" (2 Pet 3:15–16). And yet, there was no movement within the Church to establish a fixed collection of her writings to parallel those of Moses and the prophets. For early

---

8 The deuterocanonical texts were not "added" to the Church's Old Testament. No, the Church had them because its earliest Jewish members brought these texts with them, as they did the other works of the Hebrew Scriptures. See Albert C. Sunderberg Jr., "The Septuagint: The Bible of Hellenistic Judaism," in Lee Martin McDonald and James A. Sanders, eds., *The Canon Debate* (Peabody, MA: Hendrickson Publishers, 2002), 80–90.

9 Of the Jewish groups mentioned above, Pharisaism was the only one to survive the fall of Jerusalem in AD 70. When their rabbis, under the leadership of Johanan ben Zakkai, reconstituted their movement in the coastal town of Jamnia, they began the process of establishing a normative biblical canon for all of Judaism. Around AD 90 we find them debating the canonical status of Ecclesiastes and the Song of Songs. The earliest rabbinic list of scriptural texts is purported to be from the second century; but it comes down to us in the Babylonian Talmud (*Baba Batra* 14b–15a), compiled ca. AD 550–600. This canon, with its roots in Pharisaism, omitted the deuterocanonical books previously used by the Essenes and Greek-speaking synagogues, which continued in use among Christians. See Jack P. Lewis, "Jamnia Revisited," in *The Canon Debate*, 146–62.

Christians the term "New Testament" referred to the Eucharist (1 Cor 11:25; Luke 22:20)—and the books that we now *refer to* as the New Testament were the works read and preached from in the Eucharistic liturgy.[10] Initially, the churches in various cities only possessed the New Testament documents composed for them or their immediate neighbors. As copies were made and began to circulate, it was natural to ask questions about the tradition that stood behind each work. New texts that vied for the Church's consideration were also being produced: the *Didache* (c. 100), the *Epistle of Barnabas* (c. 100), the *Gospel of Peter* (c. 100), the *Apocalypse of Peter* (c. 125), *Protoevangelion of James* (c. 130–150), etc.

The question of which books should be recognized as inspired and used for teaching within the liturgy was, in a sense, foisted upon the Church by the heretic Marcion (c. 144). Marcion taught that the Father of Jesus was a different God than the one revealed in the Hebrew Scriptures; because of this he rejected the Old Testament *in toto*. He proposed a biblical canon consisting of a truncated version of Luke's Gospel and ten of Paul's epistles.[11] The bishops of the Church were understandably aghast at Marcion's proposal. It was at that point that Christians began proposing lists of which books should be admitted into the liturgy.

The first such list, the *Muratorian Canon*, is thought to have emerged in Rome sometime between AD 155–200. This list, the product of an anonymous author, was more extensive than Marcion's, but still omitted a number of works found in today's NT: James, Hebrews, 1 and 2 Peter, and 3 John. In their place, it endorsed the *Apocalypse of Peter*. If this canon did issue from Rome, James's absence is curious, given the epistle's importance to Clement and Hermas. The record of James's use in the Western Church falls silent for more than a hundred years—up until AD 308, when Pope Marcellus, in his *Letter to the Bishops in the Province of Antioch*, quoted James 3:1–8 as the words of the "Apostle James."[12]

---

[10] Scott Hahn, *Consuming the Word: The New Testament and the Eucharist in the Early Church* (New York: Image, 2013), 10.

[11] William R. Farmer and Denis M. Farkasfalvy, *The Formation of the New Testament Canon: An Ecumenical Approach* (New York: Paulist Press, 1983), 136–41; Lee Martin McDonald, *The Biblical Canon: Its Origin, Transmission, and Authority* (Grand Rapids, MI: Baker Academic, 2007), 321–33.

[12] Johnson, *Brother of Jesus*, 96.

Fortunately, during that interim we begin finding evidence of James's use in the East. Clement, the director of the school of catechumens in Alexandria, Egypt, put forward a biblical canon in his *Sketches* (c. 200).[13] He included James among the Church's inspired writings along with the other twenty-six books making up today's New Testament, but Clement did not stop there. His canon also includes the *Apocalypse of Peter* and *Epistle of Barnabas*. His successor at the school of catechumens, Origen, Christianity's first great biblical scholar, included James in what may be his own attempt at a canon (c. 250).[14] Origen has the distinction of being the first Christian writer to cite the Epistle of James by name, calling it "divine scripture" and identifying its author as an "apostle" and "brother" of the Lord.[15]

If we shift our gaze further east, to Palestine, we find the father of Church history, Bishop Eusebius of Caesarea, describing the state of the canon around AD 300. In Book Three of his *Ecclesiastical History* he identified writings as falling into one of three categories: accepted, disputed, and spurious. James was in the second: "Among the disputed books, which nevertheless are known to most, there are extant Epistles said to be of James, and Jude, and the second of Peter; and the second or third attributed to John."[16] Even if James was disputed, Eusebius himself recognized its inspiration and quoted it, in his *Commentary on the Psalms*, as the words of "the holy apostle."[17]

Also in Palestine, St. Cyril of Jerusalem included James among the canonical books when he delivered his *Catechetical Lectures* (c. 350). Cyril's canon contained twenty-six books; only the Apocalypse of John was omitted. Scholars point out that Cyril quoted from James more than from any other Greek writer — 124 times![18]

---

13 This work has survived only in fragments. Eusebius of Caesarea recounts the canonical list provided in Clement's *Sketches* in his fifth-century *History of the Church*, Book 6, chapter 14. See Jurgens, *Faith of the Early Fathers*, 1:11.
14 Homily 7 in Origen, *Homilies on Joshua*, trans. Barbara J. Bruce (Washington, DC: The Catholic University of America Press, 2002), 74–75. The books listed by Origen appear to match today's NT canon, minus the Book of Revelation.
15 Johnson, *Brother of Jesus*, 65–66. Johnson cites Origen's *Commentary on John*, Book 19, chapter 6; *Commentary on the Epistle to the Romans*, Book 4, chapters 1 and 8; and *Homilies on Leviticus*, Homily 2.
16 Jurgens, *Faith of the Early Fathers*, 1:293.
17 Johnson, *Brother of Jesus*, 87.
18 Ibid., 70.

In AD 363, around thirty bishops gathered in southwestern Turkey for the local Council of Laodicea. Together, they issued a canon mirroring Cyril of Jerusalem's. It was the first time that a *gathering of bishops* had addressed the issue of the canon; and when they did, James was included.[19]

An aberration then arises in the historical record. The general thrust in the canon's development, up until that point, had been expansion. The *Cheltenham Canon*,[20] written in Africa c. 360, went in the opposite direction. Its canon omitted James, as well as Hebrews, 2 Peter, 2 and 3 John, and Jude.[21]

The great watershed moment in the history of the New Testament was St. Athanasisus's *Thirty-Ninth Festal Letter*. As the Bishop of Alexandria, Egypt, the great champion of orthodoxy made it his practice to write Easter letters to his flock. The one penned in the spring of 367 was the first time that all twenty-seven books of the New Testament—and only those twenty-seven books—were listed together. Athanasius wrote, "These are the fountains of salvation at which they who thirst may be satisfied with the words they contain. *Only in these* is the teaching of piety proclaimed. Let no man add to these nor take away from them."[22]

At that point, the canon—and James's places within it—was quickly solidified throughout the Church universal. In 382, the *Decree of Damasus*, also part of the *Acts of the Council of Rome*, was published. In it the Bishop of Rome, then Damasus, finally made his voice heard on "what [books] the universal Catholic Church accepts and what [books] she must shun"—delineating today's canon of twenty-seven books. Damasus also charged Jerome, the greatest biblical scholar of antiquity, to revise the earlier Latin translations of Scripture according to the Greek and Hebrew text. The result was the Latin Vulgate. When Jerome translated the New Testament he ascribed the Epistle of James to the Apostle James (the Less), whom he likewise identified as one of Christ's cousins.

---

19 In hindsight it is ironic that the Council of Laodicea failed to include the Book of Revelation among the inspired books; the church in Laodicea was one of the seven to whom John addressed the work (Rev 3:14–22)!
20 Also known as the *Mommsen Canon*.
21 Alexander Souter, *The Text and Canon of the New Testament* (New York: Charles Scribner's Sons, 1913), 212–13.
22 Jurgens, *Faith of the Early Fathers*, 1:342.

At the same time, the African bishops gathered for the Council of Hippo (393) and published a twenty-seven-book canon of the New Testament. In 397, the newly-ordained Bishop of Hippo, St. Augustine, published his *On Christian Doctrine*, wherein he reiterated the canon of Hippo. This same canon was affirmed by the Council of Carthage (419), a gathering of over two hundred bishops, Augustine among them. The council ruled that, "besides the Canonical Scriptures nothing be read under the name of divine Scripture. The Canonical Scriptures are as follows," and then went on to list the forty-six books of the Old Testament and twenty-seven of the New, concluding, "For the confirmation of this canon, the church across the sea [i.e., Rome] is to be consulted."[23] Pope Boniface's subsequent approval of the council's directives settled the question of the canon for the next thousand years.

THE PROTESTANT REFORMATION

In the early sixteenth century, questions began being asked about the authorship of the Epistle of James. The printing press had been invented; and Erasmus of Rotterdam, the great humanist scholar, published his *Novum Testamentum* (1516). It was a cautious revision of Jerome's Latin, placed side-by-side with the Greek text. Erasmus, while not denying James's inspiration, did bring the epistle's apostolic origin into question. He doubted that a Jewish apostle could have been so proficient in Greek.[24] The Dominican exegete, Cardinal Cajetan, also expressed doubts regarding apostolic authorship.

Martin Luther went much further. In his German translation of the NT (1522), Luther placed James, Jude, Hebrews, and Revelation at the end of the NT, noting how they had a "different reputation" from the "true and certain chief books."[25] Calling James an "epistle of straw," Luther opined that it could not have been the work of the Apostle James.[26] In his preface to the epistle he gave his reasons:

---

[23] Quoted in Johnson, *Brother of Jesus*, 100.
[24] Douglas J. Moo, *The Letter of James* (Grand Rapids, MI: Eerdmans, 2000), 5.
[25] *Luther's Works*, Volume 35 (St. Louis: Concordia, 1963), 394.
[26] Luther denied that the epistle was written by the Apostle James (the Greater), *the Son of Zebedee*. I am unfamiliar with anyone in antiquity making such an identification. The Fathers of the Church identified the author with James, the brother of the Lord, who some went on to identify as also being one of the Twelve Apostles, James "the Less."

> In the first place it is flatly against St. Paul and all the rest of Scripture in ascribing justification to works.... This fault, therefore, proves that this epistle is not the work of any apostle. In the second place its purpose is to teach Christians, but in all this long teaching it does not once mention the Passion, the resurrection, or the Spirit of Christ.... Now it is the office of a true apostle to preach of the Passion and resurrection and office of Christ, and to lay the foundation for faith in him.... And that is the true test by which to judge all books, when we see whether or not they inculcate Christ.... [The author] wanted to guard against those who relied on faith without works, but was unequal to the task in spirit, thought, and words. He mangles the Scriptures and thereby opposes Paul and all Scripture.... Therefore, I will not have him in my Bible to be numbered among the true chief books, though I would not thereby prevent anyone from including or extolling him as he pleases, for there are otherwise many good sayings in him. One man is no man in worldly things; how, then, should this single man alone avail against Paul and all the rest of Scripture?[27]

When Luther revised his preface to James in 1530, he removed the final two sentences of the above quotation and his comment that James opposed Paul and the rest of Scripture. His other criticisms stood, and Luther continued to place James in an appendix to the New Testament.

For Luther, salvation by "faith alone" *was* the gospel, and whatever in Scripture did not agree with his conclusion was deficient by varying degrees. (The great irony is that the only time the phrase "faith alone" actually appears in the NT is James 2:24, "a man is justified by works and not by faith alone.") Lutheran scholar Paul Althaus relates how Luther deemed John's Gospel and First Epistle, the First Epistle of Peter, and the letters of Paul—especially Romans, Galatians, and Ephesians—to be the "heart and core" of Scripture. They formed a "canon within the canon."[28] Although Luther, later in life, preached from James when it arose in the lectionary, in a polemic against those

---

27 *Luther's Works*, 35:395–96.
28 Paul Althaus, *The Theology of Martin Luther* (Philadelphia: Fortress Press, 1966), 83.

who would not accept his interpretation, he quipped, "Away with James. I almost feel like throwing Jimmy into the stove..."[29]

Providentially, Luther's objections to James were not shared by the other Protestant Reformers. John Calvin agreed that James was rather sparing in his proclamation of grace, but he accepted its apostolic authority and argued that its perspective on justification could be harmonized with Paul's.[30] Ulrich Zwingli held that the Apostle James was the author and that the epistle was of equal authority to those of Paul.[31] Philip Melancthon, even though a close collaborator with Luther, shared Calvin and Zwingli's opinion that James could be reconciled with the Protestant interpretation of Paul. James, as well as Jude, Hebrews, and Revelation, maintained their rightful place in the canon. Tragically, the Reformers did join Luther in relegating the seven deuterocanonical books of the Old Testament to an appendix, wrongly assuming that the OT canon adopted by Rabbinic Judaism was more ancient than that of the Septuagint, which had been used in the Church since the days of the apostles.

The Catholic Church responded to the biblical tumult at the fourth session of the Council of Trent (April, 1546). A hundred years before, in the Ecumenical Council of Florence's *Bull of Union with the Copts*, the Church had reiterated its traditional canons of the Old and New Testaments. At Trent, however, she publicly, infallibly proclaimed the Old Testament canon of forty-six books and the New Testament canon of twenty-seven. Further, she invoked the penalty of excommunication upon those who taught otherwise until such time as they repented of their error.[32] At a later session of the council, the pope and bishops invoked the Epistle of James in their decree on the sacrament of the anointing of the sick. It is extremely rare for the Church to issue a definitive interpretation of a passage of Scripture, but it stated unequivocally that in James 5:14 the sacrament was announced to the faithful by "James the Apostle and brother of the Lord."[33]

---

29 Timothy George, "A Right Strawy Epistle: Reformation Perspectives on James," *The Southern Baptist Journal of Theology* 4/3 (Fall 2000): 23.
30 Ibid., 25.
31 Ibid.
32 The practice of excommunication has been practiced from the time of the apostles. See Mt 18:17–18; 1 Cor 5:1–13; 2 Cor 2:5–11.
33 Council of Trent, Session XIV, *The Doctrine of the Sacrament of Extreme Unction*, 1, https://www.ewtn.com/catholicism/library/fourteenth-session-of-the-council-of-trent-1480.

The Epistle's Inclusion in the New Testament

CANONICAL CONCLUSIONS

This brief history of James's acceptance among Christians serves as a case study in the assembly of the New Testament. Originally addressed to Jewish Christians, it was recopied and carried by hand to distant communities (composed of Jews and Gentiles) such as Rome and Alexandria. Over the next two hundred years some who received the epistle questioned its provenance. Some held it in suspicion, while others rejected it outright. Those bishops in whose churches James had been handed down as an apostolic work and proclaimed in the liturgy gave authoritative witness to the tradition they had received. That witness was accepted by their brother bishops and a consensus was reached. In union with their head, the Bishop of Rome, the bishops delineated which books were to be regarded as Scripture in the Church. The bishops' apostolic authority was the Holy Spirit's instrument for giving the canon of Scripture to the faithful.[34]

That has serious repercussions for anyone who looks to the Bible as a source of faith, especially those not in formal communion with the Catholic Church. I say this because all of the key figures in the formation of the canon of Scripture were also unabashedly Catholic. They taught that the bishops were the successors of the apostles (Clement of Rome,[35] Hermas,[36] Clement of Alexandria,[37] Origen,[38] Athanasius,[39] Jerome,[40] Augustine[41]); that the bread and wine of the Eucharist are transformed into Jesus's body and blood, making present Christ's sacrifice (Clement of Rome,[42] Clement of

---

34 The Christian's dependence upon the Church for the texts of Scripture of course extends much further than the canon. No one living today received the biblical texts from the hands of their original authors. Today's reader is dependent upon a chain of fellow human beings stretching back thousands of years and reaching across continents. Moreover, if we read Scripture in any language besides the original Hebrew, Aramaic, and Greek in which the texts were inspired, then we are dependent upon yet other members of the Church to interpret its meaning.
35 *Letter to the Corinthians* 42:1–4; 44:1–3.
36 *The Shepherd*, Visions 2, 4, 3.
37 *Who is the Rich Man That Shall Be Saved?*, 42.
38 *Commentary on Matthew*; *The Fundamental Doctrines* 1, Preface, 2.
39 *Four Letters to Serapion of Thmuis* 1, 28.
40 *Letters* 14:8.
41 *Against the Letter of Mani Called "The Foundation"* 4:5.
42 *Letter to the Corinthians* 44:4.

Alexandria,[43] Origen,[44] Cyril of Jerusalem,[45] Athanasius,[46] Augustine[47]); that serious sin must be confessed to God through the ministry of the presbyters (Origen,[48] Athanasius,[49] Augustine,[50] Jerome[51]); that final salvation was a matter not just of faith, but of works (Clement of Alexandria,[52] Origen,[53] Augustine[54]); and that the souls of the dead often require further purification and that they benefit from our prayers (Cyril of Jerusalem,[55] Augustine[56]). None of these great lights saw opposition between such beliefs and the teaching of Scripture, since all flowed from the same apostolic source. All of these beliefs were integral to Christianity long before congregations were equipped with a twenty-seven-book New Testament!

Whenever a Christian recognizes the New Testament as a closed, fixed body of literature, he implicitly acknowledges the Catholic bishops' authority to speak for Christ. And if the bishops spoke on Christ's behalf to recognize the canon of Scripture, then on what grounds do we deny their authority to correctly interpret Scripture and address questions of doctrine? Saint Augustine pointed this out in the fourth century to the Manichæan heretics with whom he debated:

> Perhaps you will read the gospel to me, and will attempt to find there a testimony to Manichæus. But should you meet with a person not yet believing the [books of the] gospel, how would you reply to him were he to say, "I do not believe"?

---

43 *Instructor of Children* 1:6.
44 *Homilies on Numbers* 7:2.
45 *Catechetical Lectures* 19, 7; 22, 1; 23, 21.
46 *Sermon to the Newly Baptized.*
47 *Explanation of the Psalms* 33:1:10; 98:9.
48 *Homilies on Luke*, 17; *On Psalm* 37, 2, 6; *Homilies on Leviticus* 2,4; 3,4. In the latter, Origen links to James 5:14–15 the public confession of sins to a presbyter.
49 *On the Gospel of Luke* 19.
50 *Explanation of the Psalms* 101:2:3; *Sermon to Catechumens on the Creed* 15, 16.
51 *Commentary on Matthew* 3:16–19; *Commentary on Ecclesiastes* 10:11.
52 *Stromateis* 6, 14, 108, 4.
53 *Commentaries on John* 19:6; *Commentary on Romans* 2, 4, 7.
54 *On Faith and Works* 14.21.
55 *Catechetical Lectures* 23, 9–10.
56 *The Care That Should Be Taken of the Dead* 1, 3; *Sermons* 172, 2.

> For my part, I should not believe the gospel except as moved by the authority of the Catholic Church. So when those on whose authority I have consented to believe in the gospel tell me not to believe in Manichæus, how can I but consent? ... If you say, "Do not believe the Catholics," you cannot fairly use the gospel in bringing me to faith in Manichæus; for it was at the command of the Catholics that I believed the gospel.[57]

We saw what happened to the Bible when Luther rejected the pope's and bishops' authority to establish the canon: an Old Testament lacking seven inspired works and a New Testament purported to have a canon within the canon. We know what happened after the Reformation wrenched Scripture from the bosom of the Church and pitted it against a millennium and a half of Christian teaching: generation upon generation of Christians separated and still separating. It does not have to be so. The solution has been with us from the beginning, "Obey your leaders and submit to them; for they are keeping watch over your souls, as men who will have to give account" (Heb 13:17). Irenaeus further expounded upon this principle in the second century:

> It is incumbent to obey the presbyters who are in the Church—those who, as I have shown, possess the succession from the apostles; those who, together with the succession of the episcopate, have received the certain gift of truth, according to the good pleasure of the Father. But [it is also incumbent] to hold in suspicion others who depart from the primitive succession, and assemble themselves together in any place whatsoever, [looking upon them] either as heretics of perverse minds, or as schismatics puffed up and self-pleasing.[58]
>
> ... Suppose there arise a dispute relative to some important question among us, should we not have recourse to the most ancient Churches with which the apostles held constant intercourse, and learn from

---

57 Augustine, *Against the Epistle of Manichæus, Called "The Fundamental"* 5:6, http://www.ccel.org/ccel/schaff/npnf104.iv.viii.vi.html.
58 Irenaeus, *Against the Heresies*, Book 4, 26:2, http://www.ccel.org/ccel/schaff/anf01.ix.vi.xxvii.html.

> them what is certain and clear in regard to the present question?[59]
>
> For it is a matter of necessity that every Church should agree with [the Roman] Church, on account of its pre-eminent authority... the very great, the very ancient, and universally known Church founded and organized at Rome by the two most glorious apostles, Peter and Paul.[60]

Every Christian who embraces the Epistle of James as the word of God owes it to himself, to herself, to embrace the shepherding of the pope and bishops that Christ used to preserve the epistle, transmit it, and testify to its apostolic origin and inspiration. If the Magisterium, the teaching authority, of the Catholic Church was God's instrument to place the text in our hands, then imagine the interpretive insights it has to share! Before we start unpacking the text of James, however, we need to lay additional groundwork regarding the author and his relation to Jesus.

---

59 Ibid., Book 3, 4:1, http://www.ccel.org/ccel/schaff/anf01.ix.iv.iv.html.
60 Ibid., Book 3, 3:2, http://www.ccel.org/ccel/schaff/anf01.ix.iv.iv.html.

CHAPTER 2

Our Author and the Family of Jesus

"James, a servant of God and of the Lord Jesus Christ,
To the twelve tribes in the Dispersion"
James 1:1

THE OLDEST ATTRIBUTION OF AUTHORship we have for the Epistle of James comes from the midthird century, from Origen, who stated that the author was James, an apostle and brother of the Lord. In this chapter we will explore how the traditional attribution fares in the light of modern scholarship. We will also see why Catholic and Orthodox Christians—not to mention the Protestant Reformers—see no conflict affirming that Jesus both had brothers and that his mother, Mary, remained a virgin for the entirety of her life.

WHAT THE EPISTLE REVEALS ABOUT ITS AUTHOR

The author identifies himself as "James, a servant of God and of the Lord Jesus." The English "James" is a translation of the Greek, *Iakobus*, and the Hebrew, *Yaqob*, or "Jacob." The people of first century Judea and Galilee were filled with messianic expectation that they would be delivered from the Romans and their kingdom restored to the glory it enjoyed under David and Solomon. That expectation increased the popularity of names from Israel's past.[1] Our author shares his name with the great patriarch Jacob, the father of Israel's Twelve Tribes, making it appropriate for him to address his letter "to the twelve tribes in the Dispersion" (1:1).

James appears to be writing at a very early date. There is no mention of the siege of Jerusalem and destruction of the Temple in AD 70. He likewise shows no knowledge of Gentiles coming to the Faith, a process which began in earnest during Paul's first missionary journey (AD 47–48). James and his readers were still very much within a Jewish milieu, as seen by his reference to meeting

---

1 John Meier, *A Marginal Jew: Rethinking the Historical Jesus,* vol. 1 (New York: Doubleday, 1991), 208.

in synagogues (2:2). The Epistle to the Hebrews, in contrast, was written prior to the destruction of Jerusalem, but after Jewish Christians had started being ostracized from the synagogue.[2] This has led many to postulate that James is the earliest NT document, written perhaps only sixteen years after the Resurrection.

Palestine is generally considered the epistle's place of origin. An early dating certainly points in that direction. There are also a number of incidental details scattered throughout the text showing that the author had firsthand knowledge of the Holy Land. Biblical scholar Luke Timothy Johnson provides a summary: James's knowledge of "the effect of the burning wind on vegetation (1:11); proximity to the dangerous sea (1:6; 4:3); the existence of salt and bitter springs (3:11); the cultivation of figs and olives and grapes (3:12); the distinctive reference to 'early and late rains' (5:7); the presence of day laborers on fields deprived of daily wages (5:4); [and] the use of the term 'Gehenna' (3:6)."[3] The final point is especially significant, as *Gehenna*—the Aramaic term for the Valley of Hinnom, outside Jerusalem—appears only in James and Christ's preaching in the synoptic gospels.[4]

The purpose of the epistle is eminently practical: teaching Christians to avoid sin and please God. It is reminiscent of Jewish wisdom literature, especially the books of Proverbs and Sirach. Echoing these earlier works, James extols God as the source of wisdom and directs readers to petition God for this gift (1:5–7; 3:13–18). He directly quotes Proverbs (Jas 4:6/Prov 3:34) and paraphrases Sirach (Jas 1:11–15/Sir 15:11–15, 20; Jas 1:19/Sir 5:11). His themes of avoiding sinful speech and just treatment of the poor are also common themes in the genre.

Like all NT documents, the epistle was written in Greek. The excellence of James's syntax and vocabulary led a number of twentieth-century commentators to conclude that it could not have been written by one of Jesus's relatives or apostles. The most up-to-date research, however, shows that Greek was prevalent throughout the Holy Land of the first century. This would have

---

[2] Shane Kapler, *The Epistle to the Hebrews and the Seven Core Beliefs of Catholics* (Kettering, OH: Angelico Press, 2016), 10–14.

[3] Luke Timothy Johnson, *The Letter of James: A New Translation with Introduction and Commentary* (New Haven, CT: Yale University Press, 1995), 120–21.

[4] *Gehenna* occurs seven times in Matthew, three in Mark, and once in Luke.

been especially true in Galilee, with its large Gentile population.[5] James may also have employed an *amanuensis*, or secretary, to refine the text.

James was a person of obvious authority in the early Church. He chastised his readers, expecting directives to be swiftly acted upon. The fact that he felt no need to identify himself beyond being "a servant of God and of the Lord Jesus," points to him being an easily recognized figure in the infant Church. The term servant, *doulos* ("slave" in Greek), denotes the author's complete submission to the will of God. Peter and Paul each identified himself as a *doulos* in the greetings of their epistles (Rom 1:1; Phil 1:1; Tit 1:1; 2 Pet 1:1), and the Septuagint had applied it to Moses (Deut 34:5; 1 Kings 8:53; Dan 9:11) and David (1 Kings 8:26; Jer 33:21; Ezek 37:25).[6] Its most exalted use was when it was applied to Christ (Phil 2:7). Jesus extended it to the apostles: "whoever would be great among you must be your servant (*diakonos*), and whoever would be first among you must be your slave (*doulos*)" (Matt. 20:26–27).

WHICH JAMES?

In the gospels we frequently encounter James, the son of Zebedee. He, along with his brother John, and Peter, formed the inner circle of the Twelve (Mk 5:37; Mt 17:1; 26:37). This James hailed from Galilee and certainly possessed the authority to draft such a letter. However, he was martyred in AD 44 (Acts 12:1–2) and, while there are scholars who date the epistle to the 40s, none argues that it was authored by the son of Zebedee.

That is because the tradition of the Church has always attributed the epistle to a different James — "the brother of the Lord."[7] We encounter him briefly in the gospels (Mt 13:55–56; Mk 6:3), where we learn that he was a Galilean who grew up in Nazareth alongside Jesus. He was the recipient of a special, post-resurrection appearance of the Lord (1 Cor 15:7). Saint Paul spoke of him, along with Peter and John, as one of the Jerusalem church's recognized "pillars" (Gal 2:9). When Peter had to flee Jerusalem (Acts 12:17), James was looked to as that church's overseer, or what Christians in later

---

5   Hartin, *James*, 22–23.
6   Moo, *James*, 48.
7   He is likely the James "the less," or "the younger," spoken of in Mark 15:40.

decades would call Jerusalem's "bishop"; for this reason we also frequently hear him referred to as James of Jerusalem.

Before we flesh James out further, however, we should address whether or not he was one of the Twelve Apostles. Jerome concluded that this brother of the Lord was the same James, the son of Alphaeus, found in lists of the Twelve (Mt 10:3; Mk 3:18; Lk 6:15; Acts 1:13). Later Catholic commentators, out of their deep respect for Jerome, followed his lead; and the identification continues even today in popular piety. The Catholic Church has never issued an authoritative statement on the matter; and with the advent of modern biblical studies, Jerome's opinion has become widely challenged by scholars.[8] Pope Benedict XVI, in his catechesis on the Twelve Apostles, noted the traditional identification of the two men, how the gospel traditions contained scant biographical information for either, and that it is a disputed point among experts.[9]

After this author's review of the arguments for and against identifying the brother of the Lord with the Apostle James (the son of Alphaeus), I see no historical means to arrive at an answer. Within the primitive Church, the term "apostle" appears to have been used of a wider group than the Twelve (1 Cor 15:5–7). When Origen identified the author of our epistle as a brother of the Lord *and* an apostle, he may have applied the title to Christ's relative in the wider sense in which it was used of St. Paul and even Barnabas (Acts 14:4, 14). Like them, James may not have been one of the Twelve; but he *was* a man to whom the Risen Christ had entrusted a mission and whom he *sent* (*apostolos* in Greek) as a minister to others.[10]

James of Jerusalem has emerged as a figure of great interest in recent decades—from NT scholarship, to the discovery of a controversial ossuary alleged to be his, straight on to conspiracy theories wherein James and the Twelve vied for power in the early Church.

---

8   Kelly Anderson and Daniel Keating, *James, First, Second, and Third John*, Catholic Commentary on Sacred Scripture series (Grand Rapids, MI: Baker Academic, 2017), 2.
9   Pope Benedict XVI, General Audience of June 8, 2006, http://w2.vatican.va/content/benedict-xvi/en/audiences/2006/documents/hf_ben-xvi_aud_20060628.html.
10 Mike Aquilina, *The Apostles and Their Times* (Manchester, NH: Sophia Institute Press, 2017), 34. Aquilina goes on to say, "[*Apostle*] describes an agent or vicar, an emissary or ambassador.... Scholars believe the word is a direct translation of the Hebrew *shaliah*; and the ancient rabbis pronounced that 'a man's *shaliah* is as himself.'"

At the very least, in the minds of most Christians, James represents a Christianity still tightly bound to the Mosaic Law, while Paul represents a Christianity free of such constraints. The problem with such a view, however, is that it is not supported by a close reading of Scripture, which requires us to adopt a more nuanced view.

Chronologically, Paul's Epistle to the Galatians is the earliest written testimony to James's life and ministry. Writing in the early 50s, Paul sought to address the confusion being visited upon Gentile converts by rival missionaries preaching a distorted gospel in which circumcision and life under the Mosaic Law were prerequisites for salvation in Christ. Paul laid out the authentic gospel—that salvation is obtained not through the Law but through faith in Christ, whose grace is infused into the believer and manifested in works of love (Gal 5:6). As proof that he was speaking the truth, Paul recounted his previous meetings with James, the Lord's brother, Peter, and John. After Paul laid out his gospel for them, he reports:

> [They] added nothing to me; but on the contrary, when they saw that I had been entrusted with the gospel to the uncircumcised, just as Peter had been entrusted with the gospel to the circumcised..., and when they perceived the grace that was given to me, James and Cephas and John, who were reputed to be pillars, gave to me and Barnabas the right hand of fellowship, that we should go to the Gentiles and they to the circumcised. (Gal 2:6–9)

James was one of the "pillars" (*stuloi* in Greek). The Septuagint frequently used the word to refer to the supports of the Tabernacle and columns in the Jerusalem Temple (1 Kings 7:15–22; 2 Chron 3:15–17).[11] Like Peter and John, James had a special function in the New Temple, the Church, which Christ was constructing (Jn 2:19; Eph 2:20–22; 1 Pet 2:5; Rev 3:12, 21:14). Earlier in Galatians, Paul seemed to identify James as an apostle (Gal 1:19).[12]

Some commentators on the Epistle to the Galatians see friction between James and Paul, but I do not believe the text warrants this view. They point to the letter's account of Peter drawing back from

---

11 Herschel Shanks and Ben Witherington III, *The Brother of Jesus* (San Francisco: Harper Collins, 2003), 119.
12 "But I saw none of the other apostles except James the Lord's brother."

table fellowship with Gentile Christians after "certain men came from James" (Gal 2:12). But Paul showed no signs of holding James responsible for the attitudes of those men, and the Acts of the Apostles shows a mutual respect and cooperation between the two.

Paul also wrote of James in his First Epistle to the Corinthians, where James's name appears as part of an ancient profession of faith:

> For I delivered to you as of first importance what I also received, that Christ died for our sins in accordance with the scriptures, that he was buried, that he was raised on the third day in accordance with the scriptures, and that he appeared to Cephas, then to the twelve. Then he appeared to more than five hundred brethren at one time, most of whom are still alive, though some have fallen asleep. *Then he appeared to James, then to all the apostles.* Last of all, as to one untimely born, he appeared also to me. (1 Cor 15:3–8)

Here again James is linked with the "apostles," which appears to be a larger group than "the twelve" in Paul's mind. It is commonly assumed that James was among Christ's "brethren" who did not believe during his earthly life (Jn 7:5) but came to faith after the Resurrection (Acts 1:14)—in James's case specifically because of this unique, post-resurrection appearance. But that is no more than an assumption; James is nowhere *named* as one of Christ's unbelieving relatives, and Jesus obviously had relatives, such as John the Baptist, who believed in him during his earthly life.

Our most substantial source of authoritative information about James is the Acts of the Apostles. His name appears there for the first time on the lips of Peter, after an angel releases the latter from prison in AD 44. Peter, breathless after running to the house of John Mark, told them of his rescue with the command to "tell this to James and to the brethren." Peter then fled the city of Jerusalem (Acts 12:17). James was obviously already well known in the community, and his being singled out by Peter indicates his leadership role. A fragment from Hegesippus (d. 180), preserved in Eusebius's *Ecclesiastical History*, states that James was the first bishop of Jerusalem.[13] Towards the end of the second

---

13 Hegesippus, *Commentaries on the Acts of the Church*, Book 5.

century, Clement of Alexandria recorded the tradition that James was ordained bishop by Peter, John, and James the Greater.[14] If that tradition is valid, then James would have assumed oversight of the church's day-to-day activities in the late 30s or early 40s.

James is woven back into the narrative of Acts five years later (AD 49), when the apostles and presbyters gather for the Council of Jerusalem (Acts 15:13–22). There, as Paul recounted in Galatians, the apostles considered the question of whether or not Gentile Christians must observe the Mosaic Law. Christ had not addressed the issue during his earthly ministry, but allowed the Holy Spirit to guide the apostles and presbyters to its resolution. "After much debate," Peter rose and reduced the gathering to silence with his conclusion that, if God had bestowed faith and the gift of the Holy Spirit upon the Gentiles apart from the Law, then they should be exempt from it; for it will be grace, not the Law, that will save Jew and Gentile (Acts 15:7–12). James then demonstrated to the assembly how Peter's words are nothing less than the fulfilment of the prophets. Beginning with a fusion of verses from the Septuagint translation, he said:

> As it is written, "After this I will return [paraphrase of Jer 12:15], and I will rebuild the dwelling of David, which has fallen; I will rebuild its ruins, and I will set it up, that the rest of men may seek the Lord, and all the Gentiles who are called by my name, says the Lord [Amos 9:11–12] who has made these things known from of old [Is 45:21]."
>
> Therefore my judgment is that we should not trouble those of the Gentiles who turn to God, but should write to them to abstain from the pollutions of idols and from unchastity and from what is strangled and from blood. For from early generations Moses has had in every city those who preach him, for he is read every Sabbath in the synagogues. (Acts 15:15–21)

This short vignette from Acts highlights James's skill as a biblical theologian and pastor of souls. His four proposed prohibitions were drawn from Leviticus 17–18, which is fascinating, because, as we shall see, the Epistle of James draws frequently from Leviticus 19.

---

14   Eusebius, *Ecclesiastical History*, 4, 2, 1.

The passages referenced here are 17:8–9, 17:10–12, 17:13, and 18:2–23, 26. They were the prohibitions placed upon Gentiles living in the midst of Israel.[15] The forty-year period following Christ's Passover was a time of transition; "the Mosaic Law was no longer binding but had not yet been externally removed by the destruction of the Temple."[16] Jewish Christians had lived their entire lives in obedience to the Torah's dietary restrictions, separating themselves from the ritually impure Gentiles.[17] To facilitate table fellowship between Jewish and Gentile converts—and ultimately the celebration of the Eucharist—James counseled that a temporary, pastoral provision be made. The apostles and presbyters adopted his suggested prohibitions and sent a decree to the Gentiles: "For it has seemed good *to the Holy Spirit and to us* to lay upon you no greater burden than the necessary things..." (Acts 15:28).

James showed himself a mediator again in AD 58, when Paul returned to Jerusalem from his third missionary journey. James and his presbyters rejoiced at the news of all that God had done among the Gentiles but, at the same time, encouraged Paul to ease the fears of the thousands of Jewish Christians who had been told that he "teach[es] all the Jews who are among the Gentiles to forsake Moses, telling them not to circumcise their children or observe the customs" (Acts 21:21). James counseled Paul to accompany four of his men who were completing the Nazirite vow (Num 6:1–21) to the temple, participate in the purification rite alongside them, and then pay for the shaving of their heads and the associated sacrifices as proof that he continued to respect the ancient customs (Acts 21:23–26). Paul did exactly as James counseled, demonstrating that, while Paul knew salvation comes through Christ and not the Law, he was not opposed—at least so long as the temple stood—to Jewish Christians externally maintaining their observance of the Torah.

Historically, we do not read of James again until the end of the first century when Jewish historian Flavius Josephus wrote *The Antiquities of the Jews*. He recorded how James met his death by

---

15 Stephen Pimentel, *Witnesses of the Messiah: On Acts of the Apostles 1–15* (Steubenville, OH: Emmaus Road Publishing, 2002), 138.
16 Ibid., 137.
17 David M. Freidenreich, "Food and Table Fellowship," in *The Jewish Annotated New Testament*, ed. Amy-Jill Levine and Marc Zvi Brettler (New York: Oxford University Press, 2011), 523.

stoning under the high priest Ananus in AD 62.[18] Ananus, who did not have the proper authorization to carry out capital punishment, was subsequently stripped by Rome of the high priesthood. Hegesippus (d. 180) provides a more elaborate account, stating that James was thrown from the parapet of the temple, stoned, and then beaten with a fuller's club. He was buried near the temple.[19]

THE FAMILY OF JESUS

Within the early Church there were two competing traditions regarding James's exact relation to Jesus. The first was that James was the Lord's cousin, with the term "brother" simply indicating a male relative. Papias of Hierapolis expressed this view in his *Exposition of the Sayings of the Lord*, written around 120 AD;[20] it became the dominant view in Western Christianity. The second tradition held that James was Christ's stepbrother, the son of Joseph and a prior, deceased wife. We find this view in the *Infancy Gospel of Mary* (c. 130–150), also known as the *Protoevangelion of James*.[21] This view was echoed by Origen[22] and came to be the view of Eastern Christianity. The element common to both was the historical memory that James was *not* Christ's brother by blood, and thus not the child of Mary and Joseph.

So what does the NT mean when it refers to James as the "brother of the Lord"? We do, after all, read how the crowd at Nazareth reacted to Jesus's preaching: "Is not this the carpenter's son? Is not his mother called Mary? And are not his brethren [*adelphoi*] James and Joseph and Simon and Judas? And are not all his sisters [*adelphai*] with us? Where then did this man get all this?" (Mt 13:55–56). The Greek terms are those normally used for siblings, but that doesn't tell us a great deal.

That is because the gospels were written in Greek *but reflect Semitic realities*. The native language of first-century Palestinian

---

18 Josephus, *The Antiquities of the Jews*, Book 20, chapter 9.
19 Hegisippus, *Memoirs*, Book 5, quoted in Eusebius, *Ecclesiastical History* 2, 23, 16–18. Text is available here: http://www.newadvent.org/fathers/250102.htm.
20 Papias, *Fragment X*, http://www.earlychristianwritings.com/text/papias.html.
21 The work claims to have been written by James shortly after the death of Herod the Great in 4 BC. The text is available here: http://www.newadvent.org/fathers/0847.htm.
22 Luigi Gambero, *Mary and the Fathers of the Church: The Blessed Virgin Mary in Patristic Thought* (San Francisco: Ignatius Press, 1999), 75.

Jews was Aramaic, and neither Aramaic nor Hebrew had a word for cousin. Such relations were referred to by the circumlocution "son of the brother of my father," or the more succinct "brother." When a bilingual Jew such as Matthew wrote in Greek, he carried over the habit of referring to close relations as brothers and sisters. He did so despite Greek having a word for cousin, *anepsios*.[23] The Septuagint provides a number of such examples where the Greek "brother" is used for a nephew (Gen 14:14), an uncle (Gen 29:15), a cousin (1 Chron 23:21–22), a kinsman (Deut 23:7), a friend (2 Sam 1:26), and an ally (Amos 1:9).[24]

How exactly was James related to Jesus? The crucifixion accounts clarify matters:

JOHN 19:25	MARK 15:40	MATT. 27:56
But standing by the cross of Jesus were his mother, and *his mother's sister, Mary the wife of Clopas*, and Mary Magdalene.	There were also women looking on from afar, among whom were Mary Magdalene, and *Mary the mother of James the younger and of Joses*, and Salome.	...among whom were Mary Magdalene, and *Mary the mother of James and Joseph*, and the mother of the sons of Zebedee.

In John's text the mother of Jesus is supported beneath the cross by her "sister," Mary the wife of Clopas. (Since it would be strange for sisters to share the same name, this Mary was likely a close relative of the Blessed Mother's, possibly a sister-in-law via Joseph.) In the parallel accounts, note how this Mary is identified as the mother of James and Joseph (Joses), two of the aforementioned brothers.[25] An aunt, two of the four brothers—it is more than coincidence. Scripturally speaking, it makes sense to identify James of Jerusalem as Christ's cousin.[26] Papias (AD 120) connected the dots in just this

---

23 Karl Keating, *Catholicism and Fundamentalism* (San Francisco: Ignatius Press, 1988), 283.
24 Ibid., 282.
25 Mk 16:1 and Lk 24:10 tell us that this same "Mary the mother of James" accompanied Mary Magdalene and Salome to the tomb on Easter morning.
26 Hegesippus, writing c. 175, identified James as well as Simon (who succeeded him as the bishop of Jerusalem) as being Jesus's *anepsion* (the technical Greek term for "cousin"), the sons of Christ's uncle, Clopas, and aunt, Mary; Eusebius, *Ecclesiastical History*, 3, 11, 1–2; cited in Brant Pitre, *Jesus and the Jewish Roots*

manner,[27] as did Hegesippus (AD 175)[28] and Jerome (AD 380).[29]

This certainly helps make sense of Christ's entrustment of Mary to the Apostle John at the foot of the Cross (John 19:26–27). If Mary had James and three other sons to care for her after Jesus's death, then our Lord's action was odd to say the least. Imagine the scandal of James's mother living in John's home as the two men ministered side-by-side in the Jerusalem church!

We can conclude that Jesus grew up in Nazareth as part of a close-knit, extended family. This was status quo for the time and place. It was a devout family that treasured its religious and cultural heritage. There is much that we remain in the dark about, such as the names of Christ's "sisters," but we know the names of his foster father, Joseph, his aunt and uncle, Mary and Clopas, and his male cousins: James, Joseph, Simon, and Judas. We also know that his mother remained a virgin until the end of her life—a truth worthy of a brief aside.

THE PERPETUAL VIRGINITY OF THE BLESSED VIRGIN MARY

Catholics, Eastern Orthodox, and even the Protestant Reformers share a belief in Mary's lifelong virginity. We saw above how there is no contradiction between this belief and Scripture. Further, it was *the* point of agreement between the differing ancient traditions regarding Christ's so-called brothers and sisters. It is a dogma that fulfills the OT's prophetic images, makes sense on a spiritual and psychological level, and illuminates the Christian understanding of marriage and celibacy.

As skilled artists, the writers of the New Testament painted Mary as the fulfillment, the embodiment, of the Ark of the Covenant. (Compare Lk 1:35 and Ex 40:34; Lk 1:39–46 and 2 Sam 6:2–16; also see Rev 11:19–12:5.) Just as the Ark was the holiest object under

---

of Mary (New York: Image, 2018), 124. Jude was either a fourth child born to this couple or the child of one of Christ's other relatives. I lean toward the latter, since, when Jude penned his own epistle, he identified himself not as the brother of Christ but as "Jude, a servant of Jesus Christ and brother of James" (1:1). The image painted by the gospels and epistles is that of a close-knit, extended family living in Nazareth. Such was the norm in the ancient world.

27 *Exposition of the Sayings of the Lord.*
28 Eusebius, *Ecclesiastical History*, 4, 22.
29 *Against Helvidius (The Perpetual Virginity of Blessed Mary)*, http://www.newadvent.org/fathers/3007.htm.

the Old Covenant, acting as God's earthly throne and a repository for the tablets of the Law, manna from heaven, and high priest's staff (Heb.9:4), so Mary was consecrated completely to the Lord and her womb was home to the one who is Word, heavenly bread, and eternal high priest. Anyone who touched the Ark, even with the best of intentions, met his death (1 Sam 6:19; 2 Sam 6:2–7). Joseph, the "just man" (Mt 1:19; Lk 2:22–24), would have recognized and respected his wife's consecration to the Lord.[30]

In fact, there is reason to believe that Joseph contracted his marriage to Mary with full knowledge that she had made a vow of virginity.[31] Gregory of Nyssa (d. 394) detected such a vow underlying Mary's unusual response at the Annunciation:

> She says... "How shall this be done, because I know not man?"... If, in fact, she had been betrothed to Joseph for the purposes of conjugal union, why would she have marveled when faced with the announcement of

---

[30] Joseph's desire to divorce Mary was likely an expression of his pious fear at drawing near to so great a mystery. Origen, for example, interpreted Mt 1:18–19 in this manner. The biblical text places Joseph's decision to divorce immediately after the statement that Mary "was found to be with child *of the Holy Spirit.*" Mary's miraculous pregnancy—and not the suspicion of unfaithfulness—was the motivating factor in Joseph seeking a quiet divorce. In fact, Joseph could not have been a "just man," as Scripture describes him, had he tried to hide a capital crime under the Mosaic Law. See John Saward, *Cradle of Redeeming Love: The Theology of the Christmas Mystery* (San Francisco: Ignatius Press, 2002), 205–6.

[31] Some have objected to the possibility of Mary taking such a vow, claiming that this would have been unheard-of in first-century Judaism. That is simply untrue. In the Torah (Num 30:13) we read that if a woman makes a vow to "deny herself" (*'annoth naphesh* in Hebrew), and her husband does not object to the vow within the day, then it shall stand. The Hebrew phrase *'annoth naphesh* is elsewhere understood to mean abstinence from sexual relations (Lev 16:29; Mishnah, Yoma 8:1); see the discussion in Pitre's *Jesus and the Jewish Roots of Mary*, 108–11. A vow to permanently abstain from sexual relations was uncommon, as it is in our own day, but we know of two Jewish sects, the Essenes in Palestine and the Therapeutae in Egypt, who practiced celibacy; see Meier, *A Marginal Jew*, 336–39. There is also reason to believe that a group of female virgins lived and served within the Jerusalem Temple; see the discussion in Scott Hahn, *Joy to the World* (New York: Image, 2014), 54–55. See also Dr. Taylor Marshall's online article, "Did Jewish Temple Virgins Exist and Was Mary a Temple Virgin?," which delves deeper into the scriptural texts cited by Hahn and provides supporting evidence from the Mishnah, http://taylormarshall.com/2011/12/did-jewish-temple-virgins-exist-and-was.html.

maternity, since she herself would have accepted becoming a mother according to the law of nature?[32]

Augustine, writing at roughly the same time but some 1,900 miles away, made the same deduction:

> Already, before [Christ] was conceived he wished to choose for himself, in order to be born, a virgin who was consecrated to God, as indicated by the words with which Mary responded to the angel, who was announcing her imminent motherhood: "How shall this be done, because I know not man?" And she certainly would not have responded in such a way if she had not already made a vow of virginity. She had become engaged because virginity had not yet become a custom among the Jews, but she had chosen a just man who would not have used violence to take away what she had vowed to God.[33]

Being the mother of God was an all-consuming vocation. Like other mothers, Mary was entrusted with her Son's well-being and development; but Mary was also called to spiritually contemplate the significance of every word and action of Jesus as her Lord, and, as he grew to manhood, to follow him as a disciple. With such a unique vocation and family dynamic, one recognizes how fitting it was for Christ to be Mary's only child. Any other child born to Mary would have felt—through no fault on her part—"cheated" of her attention. That was not God's plan for the Holy Family.[34]

The marriage of Mary and Joseph pointed beyond itself to the mystery of God's nuptial union with his people. Their virginity, far from casting aspersions on the marital act, points to its ultimate fulfilment in the soul's union with God in eternity. Marriage is, after all, a *sacrament*, a "great mystery" pointing beyond itself "to Christ and the church" (Eph 5:32). But as mighty as the sacraments are, they belong to the present age and will be unnecessary in the new creation (Mt 22:30; 1 Cor 13:12–13; Rev 21:22). Through

---

32   *In Nativitate Domini*, quoted in Brian K. Reynolds, *Gateway to Heaven: Marian Doctrine and Devotion, Image and Typology in the Patristic and Medieval Periods* (Hyde Park, NY: New City Press, 2012), 94.
33   *De Sancta Virginitate*, 4, 4, in Reynolds, 97.
34   For further scriptural and patristic arguments in defense of Mary's perpetual virginity, see Saward, *Cradle of Redeeming Love*, 169–233.

their marital union of hearts, but not bodies, Mary and Joseph made present the mystery to which each of us is invited; and their marriage was made fruitful in a way beyond all imagination—the coming into the world of the God-man, in their own family.[35]

The celibate vocation has been with the Church since its beginning, bearing fruit in priestly and consecrated lives of service. Jesus and Paul urged all to whom God offered this gift to embrace it (Mt 19:12; 1 Cor 7:7–8, 32–35).[36] And as with Mary and Joseph, the Lord promises supernatural fruitfulness: "Truly I tell you, there is no one who has left house or wife or brothers or parents or children, for the sake of the kingdom of God, who will not get back very much more in this age, and in the age to come eternal life" (Lk 18:29–30).

When I think of how Mary offered herself to the Lord—body and soul—my mind goes to the words of St. Paul: "I appeal to you therefore, brethren, by the mercies of God, to *present your bodies as a living sacrifice*, holy and acceptable to God, which is your *spiritual* worship" (Rom 12:1). Unsurprisingly, Paul finds himself in complete agreement with the Epistle of James and its author's conviction that "a man is justified by works and not by faith alone" (Jas 2:24)!

---

35 Christopher West, *Good News About Sex and Marriage* (Ann Arbor, MI: Servant Publications, 2000), 166–67.

36 It is worth noting that the first great attack upon belief in Mary's perpetual virginity, by Helvidius (c. 380), was also an attack upon the high esteem in which the Church held the virginal state. See Jerome's *Against Helvidius*, http://www.newadvent.org/fathers/3007.htm.

CHAPTER 3

Salvation—A Synergy of Faith and Works

> "For as the body apart from the spirit is dead, so faith apart from works is dead."
>
> James 2:26

THE EPISTLE OF JAMES IS BEST KNOWN FOR its insistence that justification, or a right relationship with God, is not a matter of faith alone. In this chapter we will allow the inspired text of James to lead us in a study of this all-important subject. We will pause periodically to bring James into conversation with Jesus, Paul, Peter, and John. In the process we will come to a more comprehensive, scriptural understanding of the roles of law, grace, faith, works, and merit in obtaining salvation. Precisely because it is scriptural, I hope this chapter will prove agreeable to Protestant and Catholic Christians alike.

We begin our examination of the topic with a lengthy quotation from James's first chapter. I wish to draw your attention to certain points through the use of italics:

> Blessed is the man who endures trial, for *when he has stood the test* he will *receive the crown of life* which God has promised to those who love him. Let no one say when he is tempted, "I am tempted by God"; for God cannot be tempted with evil and he himself tempts no one; but each person is tempted when he is lured and enticed by his own desire. Then desire when it has conceived gives birth to sin; *and sin when it is full-grown brings forth death. Do not be deceived, my beloved brethren.*
>
> Every *good endowment and every perfect gift is from above*, coming down from the Father of lights with whom there is no variation or shadow due to change. Of his own will *he brought us forth by the word of truth* that we should be a kind of first fruits of his creatures.

> Know this, my beloved brethren. Let every man be quick to hear, slow to speak, slow to anger, for the anger of man does not work the righteousness of God. Therefore *put away all filthiness* and rank growth of wickedness *and receive with meekness the implanted word*, which is *able to save your souls. But be doers of the word, and not hearers only, deceiving yourselves.* For if any one is a hearer of the word and not a doer, he is like a man who observes his natural face in a mirror; for he observes himself and goes away and at once forgets what he was like. But he who looks into *the perfect law, the law of liberty*, and *perseveres*, being no hearer that forgets but a doer that *acts, he shall be blessed in his doing.*
>
> If any one thinks he is religious, and *does not bridle his tongue* but *deceives his heart*, this man's religion is *vain*. Religion that is pure and undefiled before God and the Father is this: to *visit orphans and widows in their affliction*, and *to keep oneself unstained* from the world. (James 1:12–27)

Law, gift from above, implanted word, able to save, withstand testing, doers of the word, deceiving yourselves, keep oneself unstained, sin brings forth death, religion that is pure — these are the themes with which James wanted his readers, wants us, to grapple. He was not writing a detailed theological treatise but a passionate letter pertaining to matters of spiritual life and death. We will need to invest a significant amount of effort if we are to arrive at a clearer understanding of justification. We should begin with the subject of law, as James speaks of it in glowing terms; while the Apostle Paul is often characterized as denying it any salvific value.

THE LAW OF LIBERTY

James tells his readers that they will be blessed if they look into "the perfect law, the law of liberty" (1:25). When "law" arises in a discussion of justification, we seem to assume automatically that the Mosaic Law is meant; but that is rash. In the immediately preceding verses James spoke of the "implanted word, which is able to save your souls." He compares the man who hears that word but doesn't act on its demands to a man who observes himself in a mirror and then immediately forgets his appearance. James moves *immediately from that simile* to, "But he who looks into the perfect law, the law of liberty, and perseveres, being no hearer that forgets but a doer that acts, he shall be blessed in his doing" (1:25). The law of liberty *is* the implanted word. It is Jesus's "word of the kingdom," which he likened to a seed that, once it finds fertile ground, yields fruit thirty, sixty, and a hundred fold (Mt 13:19, 23). James's implanted word is also identical with Paul's "word of faith" that is believed in the heart and confessed with the lips (Rom 10:8–10). This law of liberty is the new covenant prophesied by Jeremiah, a law written upon the heart (Jer 31:31–33)!

James appeals to this law of liberty, this law promulgated by Christ in the hearts of his people through the gift of the Spirit, in the very next verses:

> My brethren, show no partiality as you *hold the faith of our Lord Jesus Christ*, the Lord of glory.... If you really fulfil the *royal law*, according to the scripture, *"You shall love your neighbor as yourself* [Leviticus 19:18]," you do well. But if you show partiality, you commit sin, and are convicted by the law as transgressors. For whoever keeps the whole law but fails in one point has become guilty of all of it. For he who said, "Do not commit adultery," said also, "Do not kill." If you do not commit adultery but do kill, you have become a transgressor of the law. So speak and so act as those who are to be judged under the law of liberty. For judgment is without mercy to one who has shown no mercy; yet mercy triumphs over judgment. (James 2:1, 8–13)

James explicates the Law of Moses in the light of Christ who came not to abolish the law and prophets but to fulfill, or complete,[1] them (Mt 5:17). Like Jesus, James sees Leviticus 19:18 as the heart of OT morality (Mt 22:39–40). James's train of thought here extends beyond Leviticus 19:18, though, to encompass Leviticus's entire nineteenth chapter. The early rabbis identified this section as the kernel of the Law, declaring "the essentials of the Torah are

---

1 This is the meaning of the Greek *plērōsai* used in Matthew.

summarized therein."[2] Leviticus 19 either quotes or paraphrases all ten commandments of the Decalogue along with forbidding partiality to the rich (Lev 19:15, Jas 2:1–4), slander (Lev 19:16; Jas 4:11), and the withholding of wages from workers (Lev 19:13; Jas 5:4). Jesus and Paul used Leviticus 19 in the same manner as James:

MATTHEW 19:17–19	ROMANS 13:8–10
"... If you would enter life, keep the commandments... You shall not murder, You shall not commit adultery, You shall not steal, You shall not bear false witness, Honor your father and mother, and, You shall love your neighbor as yourself."	... [H]e who loves his neighbor has fulfilled the law. The commandments, "You shall not commit adultery, You shall not kill, You shall not steal, You shall not covet," and any other commandment, are summed up in this sentence, "You shall love your neighbor as yourself." Love does no wrong to a neighbor; therefore love is the fulfilling of the law.

James calls Leviticus 19:18 the royal (*basilikon*) law for a good reason; it is the law of Christ's kingdom (*basileia*). James is not proposing the Mosaic Law as the source of his readers' salvation. Rather, he is explicating the newly-completed-law, i.e., the teachings of Christ (Mt 5:17; Jn 13:34).[3] We see this illustrated later in the epistle when James again combines talk of the law with statements from Jesus's earthly teaching:

> Do not speak evil against one another, brethren [Mt 5:23]. He that speaks evil against a brother or judges his brother, speaks evil against the law and judges the law.

---

2 *Sifra*, quoted in J. H. Hertz, ed., *The Pentateuch and Haftorahs: Hebrew Text and Commentary*, second ed. (London: Soncino Press, 1960), 497.

3 We can see this in Jas 2:11 already quoted, where James cites the first two commandments addressed by Jesus in the Sermon on the Mount: "You have heard that it was said to the men of old, '*You shall not kill*; and whoever kills shall be liable to judgment.' But I say to you that every one who is angry with his brother shall be liable to judgment; whoever insults his brother shall be liable to the council, and whoever says, 'You fool!' shall be liable to the hell of fire.... You have heard that it was said, '*You shall not commit adultery.*' But I say to you that every one who looks at a woman lustfully has already committed adultery with her in his heart" (Mt 5:21–22, 27–28).

But if you judge the law, you are not a doer of the law but a judge. There is one lawgiver and judge, he who is able to save and destroy [Mt 10:28]. But who are you that you judge your neighbor [Mt 7:1]? (James 4:11–12)

Christ calls us to go beyond outward obedience to a command. He demands deep, interior conversion. James likened the law of Christ to a mirror into which we, who were made in the image and likeness of God, can gaze and see our true reflection (Gen 1:27; Jas 3:9; 1:23–25). The Son is the perfect reflection of the Father, and we, *united to him*, are called to become "perfect as [our] heavenly Father is perfect" (Mt 5:48). We do this by *acting upon* what we have seen (Jas 1:22). And this is possible because, unlike the Law of Moses, Christ is able to reach inside of us and, by grace, bring about an interior transformation. He empowers us to break free of sinful behaviors and persevere despite temptation.[4]

FIRST EXCURSUS: INITIAL JUSTIFICATION

James has touched upon the beginnings of our life in Christ. We should pause to flesh out the Church's teaching before going further in our study. We need to bring James into conversation with the gospel accounts of Jesus's teaching and the other NT writings.

The Triune God is the source of our justification. "God has done what the law [of Moses], weakened by the flesh, could not do: sending his own Son in the likeness of sinful flesh and as a sin offering" (Rom 8:3). We are invited to share Jesus's resurrected life, and this through no merit on our part.[5] Faith in Christ's divinity and his paschal mystery is planted in our hearts by the Spirit (Mt 16:17; 1 Cor 12:3).[6] This faith is the *beginning*, "the foundation

---

4 "By him every one that believes is freed from everything from which you could not be freed by the law of Moses" (Acts 13:39).

5 The Catholic Church could not be more emphatic on this point: "[N]one of the things that precede justification, whether by faith or works, merit the grace of justification. For, if by grace, it is not now by works, otherwise, as the Apostle says, grace is no more grace [Rom 11:6]." Council of Trent, *Decree Concerning Justification*, 7, https://www.ewtn.com/catholicism/library/decree-concerning-justification--decree-concerning-reform-1496.

6 "It is furthermore declared that in adults the beginning of that justification must proceed from the predisposing grace of God through Jesus Christ, that is, from His vocation, whereby, without any merits on their part, they are called; and they who by sin had been cut off from God, may be disposed through the

and root," of our justification.[7] The Apostle John wrote, "to all who received [Jesus], who *believed* in his name, he gave power to *become* children of God" (Jn 1:12). Faith is an absolute necessity; the Epistle to the Hebrews says bluntly, "without faith it is impossible to please [God]" (Heb 11:6).

This faith must be acted upon. Peter made clear, on the day of Pentecost, how faith comes to fruition. When asked by the crowd what they must do to be saved, he answered, "Repent, and be baptized every one of you in the name of Jesus Christ for the forgiveness of your sins; and you shall receive the gift of the Holy Spirit" (Acts 2:38). Peter echoed the Lord Jesus: "Truly, truly, I say to you, unless one is born of water and the Spirit, he cannot enter the kingdom of God" (Jn 3:5).

Baptism transforms us from creatures of God into beloved children. It is where we make our confession of faith (Rom 10:9; 1 Tim 6:12). As the minister intones the words, "I baptize you in the name of the Father and of the Son and of the Holy Spirit" (cf. Mt 28:19), the Holy Spirit rushes into our souls, making us sons in the Son. Peter wrote that we are "born anew, not of perishable seed but of imperishable" (1 Pet 1:23), and called to become "partakers of the divine nature" (2 Pet 1:4).[8] This is so far beyond our human nature, so far beyond anything we could *possibly* merit for ourselves, that justification could never be anything but a gift.

Baptism was far more than a symbolic act in the minds of the apostles. The God who created matter freely employs it to communicate his grace:

> When the goodness and kindness of God our Savior appeared, he saved us, not because of deeds done by us in righteousness, but in virtue of his own mercy, *by the washing of regeneration and renewal in the Holy Spirit*, which he poured out upon us richly through Jesus Christ

---

quickening and helping grace to convert themselves to their own justification by freely assenting to and cooperating with that grace." Ibid., 5.

[7] Ibid., 8.

[8] Justification is "not only a remission of sins but also the sanctification and renewal of the inward man through the voluntary reception of the grace and gifts whereby an unjust man becomes just and from being an enemy becomes a friend, that he may be an heir according to hope of everlasting life [Tit. 3:7]." Council of Trent, *Decree Concerning Justification*, 7.

our Savior, so that we might be *justified by his grace* and become heirs *in hope of eternal life.* (Tit 3:4–7)

[God] waited in the days of Noah, during the building of the ark, in which a few, that is, eight persons, were saved through water. *Baptism, which corresponds to this, now saves you.* (1 Pet 3:20–21)

This would not have shocked the Jewish people. It was a literal fulfillment of Ezekiel's prophecy of the New Covenant: "I will sprinkle clean water upon you, and you shall be clean...and I will take out of your flesh the heart of stone and give you a heart of flesh. And I will put my spirit within you, and cause you to walk in my statutes" (Ezek 36:25–27). Physical circumcision is no longer incumbent upon the Christian because baptism circumcises the heart, washing away original sin (Col 2:11–13; Rom 2:26–29; Rom 5:12–19), and uniting us to the Person of Christ. Jesus is the vine, and we are the branches sharing his life (Jn 15:5). Christ is the head, and we are the body (1 Cor 12:12). It is no longer we who live, but Christ who lives in us (Gal 2:20). With the above truths fresh in our minds we are in a better position to proceed with the text of James.

JAMES'S INSISTENCE ON WORKS

We turn now to the best-known section of James's letter, the portion that Luther judged to be in direct opposition to St. Paul. James builds upon his earlier statement that believers in Christ must be "doers of the word, and not hearers only" (1:22):

What does it profit, my brethren, if a man says he has faith but has not works? Can his faith save him? If a brother or sister is poorly clothed and in lack of daily food, and one of you says to them, "Go in peace, be warmed and filled," without giving them the things needed for the body, what does it profit? So faith by itself, if it has no works, is dead. (2:14–17)

James's thought is very close to the Apostle John's: "But if any one has the world's goods and sees his brother in need, yet closes his heart against him, how does God's love abide in him? Little children, let us not love in word or speech but in deed and in truth" (1 John 3:17–18). It also recalls the criteria that Jesus gave for the final judgment: "Come, O blessed of my Father, inherit the kingdom prepared for you from the foundation of the world; for I was hungry and you gave me food... I was naked and you clothed me" (Mt 25:34–36). Faith that is not translated into action is useless. James continues:

> But some one will say, "You have faith and I have works." Show me your faith apart from your works, and I by my works will show you my faith. You believe that God is one; you do well. Even the demons believe—and shudder. (James 2:18–19)

A faith that is merely an intellectual assent benefits a man no more than it does a demon.

James's teaching agrees with the concept of faith extolled in the Epistle to the Hebrews. Its author, after defining faith as "the assurance of things hoped for, the conviction of things not seen" (Heb 11:1), recounts numerous believers who accomplished amazing works "by faith." We are told, for example, "By faith Noah, being warned by God concerning events as yet unseen, took heed and constructed an ark for the saving of his household" (Heb 11:7) The implication is that had Noah not acted upon his faith, he and his family would have perished in the deluge. Like the author of Hebrews, James proceeds to bolster his argument with examples, citing two individuals who also appear in Hebrews—Abraham and Rahab:

> Do you want to be shown, you foolish fellow, that faith apart from works is barren? Was not Abraham our father justified by works, when he offered his son Isaac upon the altar? You see that faith was active along with his works, and faith was completed by works, and the Scripture was fulfilled which says, "Abraham believed God, and it was reckoned to him as righteousness"; and he was called the friend of God. You see that a man is justified by works and not by faith alone. And in the same way was not also Rahab the harlot justified by works when she received the messengers and sent them out another way? For as the body apart from the spirit is dead, so faith apart from works is dead. (James 2:20–26)

James's choice of terms is instructive. When Abraham offered Isaac his faith was "active [*synērgei*] along with his works, and faith was completed [*teleioō*] by works" (2:22). *Synērgei*, from which we receive our English word "synergy," means to "work with"; and *teleioō* means "to complete, to bring to perfection or maturity." Faith both inspired Abraham's works and was active along with them, and *in that interaction* faith was brought to completion and maturity!9

James quotes the famous passage from Genesis 15:6 where Abraham, who had already "by faith" left his homeland, received God's promise that, even though he was close to eighty years old, he would have descendants as numerous as the stars. Abraham's faith in God's promise was "reckoned to him as righteousness." James, taking a cue from 1 Maccabees 2:52,10 tells us that Genesis 15:6 was fulfilled [*plēroun*] when Abraham placed Isaac upon the altar. *Plēroun* is the term used throughout the NT for the fulfillment of a prophetic word.11 James is saying that, through works, Abraham's faith reached the end for which God had always intended it: a life of righteousness, or justification.

The example of Abraham leads James to the declaration "You see that a man is justified by works and not by faith alone" (2:24). Together, faith and the works that faith inspires effect a true *synergy*—a result impossible to either if left to itself. For the Christian, faith that fails to find expression in works will prove to be as ineffectual as a body without spirit. But faith that is perseveringly united to works will result in our final justification before Christ's judgment seat.

SECOND EXCURSUS: PROGRESS IN JUSTIFICATION

Luther famously saw conflict between James's "a man is justified by works and not by faith alone," and Paul's "a man is justified by faith apart from works of law" (Rom 3:28). This would seem compounded by Paul's quotation of Genesis 15:6; but the difficulty is only apparent. The agreement exhibited by Paul and James at the Council of Jerusalem extends to their epistles as well.

---

9   Hartin, *James*, 159.
10 "Was not Abraham found faithful when tested, and it was reckoned to him as righteousness?"
11 Johnson, *James*, 243. Jesus used the same term when he said that he came to "fulfill" the law (Mt 5:14).

James wrote to Jewish Christians who he had reason to believe were lax in living their faith. Paul's Epistle to the Romans, on the other hand, was written to a mixed community in which Jewish believers insisted that Gentiles who came to faith in Christ were not truly justified until they were circumcised and began living under the Mosaic Law's extensive cultic and dietary stipulations. Paul countered this by pointing out that Abraham was justified because of his faith in God's promise (Rom 4:3; Gen 15:6) — before the covenant of circumcision (Gen 17:24) and four hundred years before the giving of the Law. Paul dealt with the question of how one is initially justified; and that process, as we have already seen, begins with faith.

Christians do live under *a law*, but it is not the Law of Moses. It is what James calls "the royal law" and what Paul calls the "law of Christ" (Gal 6:2; 1 Cor 9:21).[12] Paul makes a distinction between "works of the law" and other "works" which must be manifest if one is to obtain final salvation:

> [God] will render to every man according to his *works*: to those who by patience in *well-doing* seek for glory and honor and immortality, *he will give eternal life*.... It is not the hearers of the [Mosaic] law who are righteous before God, but the doers of the law who will

---

[12] "A significant portion of Christ's law is God's eternal law, or what philosophers and theologians call natural law. The tenets of the natural law are discernible by reason and incumbent upon every human conscience. We find its prohibitions reflected across cultures (the condemnation of murder, adultery, treason, theft), although because of sin's power to distort the intellect, aberrations appeared (e.g., acceptance of polygamy, infanticide, euthanasia). To counter such errors God explicitly reiterated the main precepts of the natural law in the Torah, in the Ten Commandments. We Christians must live by these commands if we are to inherit eternal life. We are bound to them, however, not because they appear in the Torah; but because they are part of God's eternal law. Paul said that he labored among the Gentiles to 'bring about the *obedience* of faith' (Rom 1:5). The Law of Christ also consist of Christ's positive commands: we must be baptized (Matt 28:19; Mark 16:16), celebrate the Eucharist (Luke 22:19–20; John 6:43–54), and obey the shepherds of his Church (Luke 10:16; Matt 18:18, 28:20; Heb 13:17). Jesus told the apostles, 'A new commandment I give to you, that you love one another, even as I have loved you' (John 13:34); and 'If you love me, you will *keep my commandments*' (John 14:15). The Law of Christ is actually far more demanding than the Torah's 613 commands," but Christ fills us with his grace and acts in us (Kapler, *Hebrews*, 70–71).

be justified. When Gentiles who have not the law [of Moses] do by nature what the law requires, they are a law to themselves, even though they do not have the law. They show that what the law requires is *written on their hearts*, while their conscience also bears witness and their conflicting thoughts accuse or perhaps excuse them on that day when, according to my gospel, God judges the secrets of men by Christ Jesus. (Rom 2:6–7, 13–16)

Gentile Christians who participate in the New Covenant, wherein the moral demands of the law (i.e., the Ten Commandments, Leviticus 19:18) are written upon the hearts by the Spirit,[13] will live moral lives (produce good works); and, as a result, obtain eternal life (final justification).[14] Paul makes the same point in Galatians: "[T]hrough the Spirit, *by faith*, we wait for the *hope of righteousness*. For in Christ Jesus neither circumcision nor uncircumcision is of any avail, but faith *working through love*" (Gal 5:5–6). There is no true conflict between Paul and James. They even make the same distinction between those who *hear* and those who *do* (Rom 2:13; James 1:22)!

If we are troubled by the thought that our actions play a significant role in obtaining final salvation, it is only because we have forgotten the all-important truth that Christ lives in us. When the Son became man, he began to do in his human nature what he had done from all eternity in his divine nature: pour himself out to the Father in the love who is the Spirit. Christ now pours himself out to the Father, and his human brothers and sisters, *through us* who are united to Him in baptism.[15] He breathes the Holy Spirit upon us, who in turn fills us with the love of God (Rom 5:5). The Spirit prays within us, moving us to cry, "Father!" (Rom 8:26–27; Gal 4:6). He inspires us with the works that, from eternity, God

---

13 Jer 31:31–33; Rom 8:1–2, 4–5.

14 "No one, however much justified, should consider himself exempt from the observance of the commandments; no one should use that rash statement, once forbidden by the Fathers under anathema, [that] the observance of the commandments of God is impossible for one that is justified." Council of Trent, *Decree on Justification*, 16.

15 "For...Christ Jesus Himself, as the head into the members and the vine into the branches [Jn 15:1], continually infuses strength into the justified, which strength always precedes, accompanies, and follows their good works, and without which they could not in any manner be pleasing and meritorious before God...." Council of Trent, *Decree on Justification*, 16.

has willed that *we* perform (Eph 1:11–12; 2:10)—and even more, he gives us the grace, the spiritual strength, to accomplish them.[16] As members of his mystical body, Jesus imparts gifts to us so that we may help build one another up.[17] The sacraments are privileged channels of grace, especially the Eucharist. (Jesus went so far as to say, "unless you eat the flesh of the Son of man and drink his blood, you have no life in you" [Jn 6:53].) Joined to Christ we become "living sacrifice[s], holy and acceptable to God" (Rom 12:1).

The works that God calls us to are not great feats but faithful, daily expressions of love. Ninety percent of Christ's earthly life was lived as a son, cousin, neighbor, apprentice, and carpenter. The people of Nazareth were shocked when he began his ministry. Up until he was baptized by John, Jesus had epitomized the quiet, holy life advocated by the prophets: to do justice, love kindness, and walk humbly with God (Mic 6:8). That was the work the Father gave him to perform throughout his first thirty years—daily, obedient love of the Father expressed through prayer, his obedience to Mary and Joseph, small sacrifices in the home, kindness shown to neighbors and the needy, attentiveness to his craft, and heartfelt forgiveness of those who wronged him. This is the life and these are the works—*Christ's life* and *Christ's works*—that must be manifest in each member of the mystical body.

Every good work originates in God but is actualized in us, and thus requires our consent and cooperation. That is why Paul told the Philippians to "work out your own salvation with fear and trembling; for God is at work in you, both to will and to work for his good pleasure" (Phil 2:12–13). Recall Jesus's parable of the talents. A man went on a journey and entrusted his three servants with varying sums of money. The first two servants invested

---

16 "His divine power has granted to us all things that pertain to life and godliness" (2 Pet 1:3); "I can do all things in him who strengthens me" (Phil 4:13); "[B]y the grace of God I am what I am, and his grace toward me was not in vain. On the contrary, I worked harder than any of them, though it was not I, but the grace of God which is with me" (1 Cor 15:10); "Having gifts that differ according to the grace given to us, let us use them" (Rom 12:6).

17 "And [Jesus] gave some as apostles, others as prophets, others as evangelists, others as pastors and teachers, *to equip the holy ones for the work of ministry*, for building up the body of Christ, until we all attain to the unity of faith and knowledge of the Son of God, *to mature manhood, to the extent of the full stature of Christ*" (Eph 4:11–13, NABRE).

what they were given, doubled it, and upon their master's return, received his praise. The third servant, however, buried the money for fear of losing it. The enraged master ordered that the third servant should *lose what had been entrusted to him* and he be cast "into the outer darkness where there will be weeping and gnashing of teeth" (Mt 25:14–30). We must put the grace we have been given to work. Jesus also likened the kingdom of heaven to a wedding feast that a king threw for his son, and to which he invited "the bad and good." When the king entered the feast and spotted a guest without a "wedding garment," he had the man bound hand and foot and thrown into the "outer darkness [where] there will be weeping and gnashing of teeth"; for "many are called but few are chosen" (Mt 22:10–14). The Apostle John revisited this imagery of the wedding garment in the Book of Revelation, where he shows us Christ's bride, the Church, clothed in "fine linen, bright and pure," representing "the righteous deeds of the saints" (Rev 19:8). John clearly remembered our Lord's parable.[18] Peter also captured the dynamic between the movement of God's grace and our cooperation. He reminded the Church:

> His divine power has granted to us all things that pertain to life and godliness.... For this very reason make every effort to supplement your faith with virtue, and virtue with knowledge, and knowledge with self-control, and self-control with steadfastness, and steadfastness with godliness, and godliness with brotherly affection, and brotherly affection with love. For *if* these things are yours and abound, they keep you from being ineffective or unfruitful in the knowledge of our Lord Jesus Christ.... Therefore, brethren, be the more zealous to *confirm your call and election*, for if you do this you will never fall; so there will be richly provided for you an entrance into the *eternal kingdom* of our Lord and Savior Jesus Christ. (2 Pet 1:3, 5–8, 10–11)

---

18 John's Gospel also records, in terms very similar to the parables of the talents and the wedding feast, Christ's words about those who do not produce good works: "I am the true vine, and my Father is the vinedresser. Every branch of mine that bears no fruit, he takes away.... the branches are gathered, thrown into the fire and burned" (Mt 25:14–30).

The author of Hebrews concurs, telling readers that God disciplines us "that we may share his holiness... the holiness without which no one will see the Lord" (Heb 12:10, 14).

Our Father is so benevolent that each small "yes" we give is rewarded with more grace, so that we may manifest even greater works of love. We are said to "merit" this increase of grace, but never in the sense that God is made our debtor. Rather, we "merit" in the same way that a child who eats everything on his plate merits a second helping.[19] God's response is predicated not upon law but upon his fatherly love![20] Our salvation, from start to finish, is the action of God—even our good works and merit.[21]

JAMES'S WARNING ABOUT DEADLY SIN

If a person professes faith in Christ but fails to exhibit Christ's life, there are reasons. It may stem from a lack of solid catechesis: a heretical understanding of God's grace[22] or lack of knowledge about the many channels of grace entrusted to the Church. More likely than not, however, sin is the culprit. Each of us encounters temptation on a daily basis. James brings this up early in his letter:

> Blessed is the man who endures trial, for *when he has stood the test* he will receive the crown of life which God has promised to those who love him. Let no one say when he is tempted, "I am tempted by God"; for God cannot be tempted with evil and he himself tempts no one;[23] but each person is tempted when he is *lured and*

---

19 Scott Hahn, *Hail Holy Queen: The Mother of God in the Word of God* (San Francisco: Doubleday, 2001), 133–34. Recall again Jesus's parable of the talents. In regards to the first two servants, who invested what they were given by the master, we are told, "For to everyone who has will more be given, and he will have an abundance" (Mt 25:29).

20 "For God is not so unjust as to overlook your work and the love which you showed for his sake in serving the saints" (Heb 6:10); "[G]ive, and it will be given to you; good measure, pressed down, shaken together, running over, will be put into your lap" (Lk 6:38).

21 "Far be it that a Christian should either trust or glory in himself and not in the Lord [1 Cor 1:31; 2 Cor 10:17], whose bounty toward all men is so great that He wishes the things that are His gifts to be their merits," Council of Trent, *Decree on Justification*, 16.

22 "What shall we say then? Are we to continue in sin that grace may abound? By no means! How can we who died to sin still live in it?" (Rom 6:1–2).

23 James appears to be drawing from Sir 15:11–12, "Do not say, 'Because of the

enticed by his own desire. Then desire when it has conceived gives birth to sin; and sin when it is full-grown *brings forth death.* (James 1:12–15)

Earlier, we read James's statement that every sin is a violation of the new law, the absolute perfection to which Christ calls us (Jas 2:10); but James also teaches that not all sin is of such gravity that it extinguishes the supernatural life within us. He demonstrates this when he says, "For we all make many mistakes, and if any one makes no mistakes in what he says he is a perfect man" (Jas 3:2). Further, there are sins of omission: "Whoever knows what is right to do and fails to do it, for him it is sin" (4:17).

In all of this, James reflects a thoroughly Jewish understanding of sin. The OT uses some twenty different designations for sin, but the rabbis taught that the three that appear most frequently refer to different degrees of sin: *het* (also appearing as *hatta'ah*, or *hattat*), the lightest, is an infraction of a command of which one is ignorant; *awon* is a knowing breach of a minor commandment, with the most serious, *pesha/resha'*, being a presumptuous or rebellious act against the Lord.[24] We find the same gradations of sin in Psalm 106:6, "Both we and our fathers have sinned [*hata'nu*]; we have committed iniquity [*he-'ewinu*], we have done wickedly [*hirsha'nu*]."[25] When the high priest entered the Holy of Holies on Yom Kippur, he confessed the nation's *het*, *awon*, and *pesha* before the Lord. It would stand to reason that when James speaks of sins that "bring forth death" (1:15) he means great transgressions, blatant rejections of God's kingship. Like James, the Apostle John recognized some sins as "mortal," or deadly (1 Jn 5:16–17).[26] The Apostle Paul provides a list of such sins:

Lord I left the right way'; for he will not do what he hates. Do not say, 'It was he who led me astray'; for he had no need of a sinful man."

24 Louis Jacobs, "Sin," *Encyclopedia Judaica* (Jerusalem: Ketter Publishing House, 1972); Joseph Jacobs and Judah David Eisenstein, "Sin," *The Jewish Encyclopedia* (1906), http://www.jewishencyclopedia.com/articles/13761-sin.

25 J. Jacobs and Eisenstein, "Sin"; Ps 19:12–13 also shows a distinction in the gravity of sin: "[W]ho can discern his errors? Clear thou me from hidden faults. Keep back thy servant also from presumptuous sins; let them not have dominion over me! Then I shall be blameless, and innocent of great transgression."

26 "If any one sees his brother committing what is not a mortal sin, he will ask, and God will give him life for those whose sin is not mortal. There is sin which is mortal; I do not say that one is to pray for that. All wrongdoing is sin, but there is sin which is not mortal" (1 Jn 5:16–17).

> Do not be deceived; neither the immoral, nor idolaters, nor adulterers, nor [practicing] homosexuals, nor thieves, nor the greedy, nor drunkards, nor revilers, nor robbers will inherit the kingdom of God. (1 Cor 6:9–10)

James is keen on addressing a couple of sins in particular: the rich person's abuse of the poor (which we will focus upon in chapter six) and sins of speech, which we will tackle here. Above, St. Paul said that "revilers," *loidoroi* in Greek, will not inherit the kingdom. The term refers to those who denigrate another's reputation. James speaks in the same vein:

> [T]he tongue is a fire. The tongue is an *unrighteous world* among our members, *staining the whole body*, setting on fire the cycle of nature, and *set on fire by hell*. For every kind of beast and bird, of reptile and sea creature, can be tamed and has been tamed by mankind, but no human being can tame the tongue—a restless evil, full of deadly poison. With it we bless the Lord and Father, and with it we curse men, who are made in the likeness of God. From the same mouth come blessing and cursing. My brethren, this ought not to be so. Does a spring pour forth from the same opening fresh water and brackish? Can a fig tree, my brethren, yield olives, or a grapevine figs? (James 3:6–12)[27]

Why are Christians, who have received the gift of the Spirit, still susceptible to such grave sins? Early in his epistle James writes that a man is tempted when he is "lured and enticed by his own desires" (1:14). He continues this train of thought in chapter four when he asks:

> What causes wars, and what causes fightings among you? Is it not *your passions that are at war in your members*? You desire and do not have; so you kill. And you covet and cannot obtain; so you fight and wage war. (James 4:1–2)

---

27 Another echo from Christ's Sermon on the Mount, "Are grapes gathered from thorns, or figs from thistles? So, every sound tree bears good fruit, but the bad tree bears evil fruit.... Every tree that does not bear good fruit is cut down and thrown into the fire" (Mt 7:16–17, 19).

James finds himself in close proximity to the rabbis who spoke of the *yezer-ha-ra*, or man's inclination to gratify his instincts;[28] and James is in perfect agreement with Paul who wrote of our struggle against "the flesh" (Rom 7:21–23; 8:12–13). Satan exploits these inclinations, targeting his temptations at those appetites to which we are most prone.

James, however, has learned the secret of emerging victorious over the flesh and the devil:

> But [God] gives more grace; therefore it says, "God opposes the proud, but gives grace to the humble" [Prov 3:34]. Submit yourselves therefore to God. Resist the devil and he will flee from you. Draw near to God and he will draw near to you. Cleanse your hands, you sinners, and purify your hearts, you men of double mind. Be wretched and mourn and weep. Let your laughter be turned to mourning and your joy to dejection. Humble yourselves before the Lord and he will exalt you. (James 4:6–10)

Our only recourse is to return to the source of our strength, God himself. We turn from our sin and draw near to God through prayer, the sacraments, our brothers and sisters in the Church, and Scripture ... and when the devil tempts us, we must maintain our "no." But we can do that only by experiencing sincere contrition for our failings, humbly seeking God's forgiveness, and then availing ourselves of the channels of grace noted above. In time, the Lord may employ us to bring back others who have wandered into sin: "My brethren, if any one among you wanders from the truth and some one brings him back, let him know that whoever brings back a sinner from the error of his way will save his soul from death and will cover a multitude of sins" (Jas 5:19–20).

THIRD EXCURSUS: VENIAL AND MORTAL SIN

In baptism the separation from God, into which every human being is born, is overcome. We are freed from the sin of Adam, reborn of God's imperishable seed, and made partakers of the divine

---

[28] L. Jacobs, "Sin"; see also W. D. Davies, *Paul and Rabbinic Judaism*, rev. ed. (New York: Harper & Row, 1967), 20–21.

nature (Rom 5:17–6:4; 1 Pet 1:23; 2 Pet 1:4). This does not, however, eliminate the consequences of humanity's fall: physical death, suffering, and an inclination toward sin, or what the Church calls *concupiscence*.[29] Concupiscence is that strong pull we feel to satiate our appetites, an "inner thirst for pleasure, power, and possessions."[30]

Faithful to her Jewish roots, the Catholic Church recognizes sins of omission and commission as well as distinctions in the gravity of sins. Less serious sins—either sins not pertaining to grave matter, or, if the matter is grave, committed in ignorance of God's eternal law, or without full consent of the will—are called *venial*. The Apostle John wrote, "All wrongdoing is sin, but there is sin which is not mortal" (1 Jn 5:17). Venial sins impede the flow of Christ's life within us but do not sever our union with the Lord. They are forgiven through prayer; that is why Christ taught us to petition the Father, "Forgive us our trespasses as we forgive those who trespass against us."[31] Venial sins are not harmless. If not repented of, and penance undertaken to undo the pattern of behavior, they lead one down the path to mortal sin; thus James's statement, "desire when it has conceived gives birth to sin; and sin *when it is full-grown* brings forth death" (1:15).

Mortal, or deadly, sins are grave violations of God's *eternal law*—the precepts of which are accessible to conscience and made explicit in the Ten Commandments (Mt 19:17–19; Rom 2:12–16).[32] Some Christians outside of the Catholic Church teach that it is not possible for an authentic Christian to succumb to mortal sin; and

---

29 "In the one baptized there remains concupiscence or an inclination to sin, which, since it is left for us to wrestle with, cannot injure those who do not acquiesce but resist manfully by the grace of Jesus Christ; indeed, he who shall have striven lawfully shall be crowned [Eph 4:22, 24; Col 3:9]. This concupiscence, which the Apostle sometimes calls sin [Rom 6–8; Col 3], the holy council declares the Catholic Church has never understood to be called sin in the sense that it is truly and properly sin in those born again, but in the sense that it is of sin and inclines to sin." Council of Trent, *Decree on Original Sin*, 5, https://www.ewtn.com/catholicism/library/decree-concerning-original-sin--decree-concerning-reform-1495.
30 Scott W. Hahn, *Romans*, Catholic Commentary on Sacred Scripture series (Grand Rapids, MI: Baker Academic, 2017), 119.
31 "For though during this mortal life, men, however holy and just, fall at times into at least light and daily sins, which are also called venial, they do not on that account cease to be just, for that petition of the just, *forgive us our trespasses* [Mt 6:12], is both humble and true," Council of Trent, *Decree on Justification*, 11.
32 *Catechism of the Catholic Church*, 1858.

while there are passages of the NT that, taken in isolation, appear to teach this, it is not the NT's overarching teaching. We read St. Paul's list of mortal sins above, but he has much more to say:

> Do you not know that in a race all the runners compete, but only one receives the prize? So run that you may obtain it. Every athlete exercises self-control in all things. They do it to receive a perishable wreath, but we an imperishable. Well, I do not run aimlessly, I do not box as one beating the air; but I pommel my body and subdue it, lest after preaching to others I myself should be disqualified. (1 Cor 9:24–27)
>
> I want you to know, brethren, that our fathers were all under the cloud, and all passed through the sea, and all were baptized into Moses in the cloud and in the sea, and all ate the same supernatural food.... Nevertheless with most of them God was not pleased; for they were overthrown in the wilderness. Now these things are warnings for us, not to desire evil as they did.... We must not indulge in immorality as some of them did, and twenty-three thousand fell in a single day.... [T]hese things happened to them as a warning, but they were written down for our instruction, upon whom the end of the ages has come. Therefore let any one who thinks that he stands take heed lest he fall. (1 Cor 10:1–3, 5–6, 8, 11–12)
>
> The works of the flesh are plain: immorality, impurity, licentiousness, idolatry, sorcery, enmity, strife, jealousy, anger, selfishness, dissension, party spirit, envy, drunkenness, carousing, and the like. I warn you, as I warned you before, that those who do such things shall not inherit the kingdom of God. (Gal 5:19–21)

Paul gave these warnings to baptized Christians, members of Christ's Church—as did the author of the Epistle to the Hebrews, St. Peter, and St. John:

> Take care, *brethren*, lest there be in any of you an evil, unbelieving heart, leading you to fall away from the living God. But exhort one another every day, as long as it is

called "today," that none of you may be hardened by the deceitfulness of sin. For we share in Christ, if only we hold our first confidence firm to the end. (Hebrews 3:12–14)

If, after they have escaped the defilements of the world through the knowledge of our Lord and Savior Jesus Christ, they are *again entangled in them and overpowered*, the last state has become worse for them than the first. For it would have been better for them never to have known the way of righteousness than after knowing it to turn back from the holy commandment delivered to them. (2 Pet 2:20–21).

He who says "I know him" but disobeys his commandments is a liar, and the truth is not in him; but whoever keeps his word, in him truly love for God is perfected. By this we may be sure that we are in him: he who says he abides in him ought to walk in the same way in which he walked. (1 Jn 2:4–6)

John went on to instruct the Church, "If any one sees his brother committing what is not a mortal sin, he will ask, and God will give him life for those whose sin is not mortal. There is sin which is mortal; I do not say that one is to pray for that" (1 Jn 5:16). It is not that such sins put one beyond God's mercy, but their healing requires sacramental confession. The Gospel of John records this sacrament's institution (Jn 20:21–23), and the early Church saw it in James 5:15–16, a subject to which we will return in chapter seven.

Christ's mercy toward us knows no bounds, and that mercy is meant to characterize the Christian. James counsels us to "act as those who are to be judged under the law of liberty," with the reminder that, "judgment is without mercy to one who shows no mercy, yet mercy triumphs over judgment" (2:12–13). James heard those words from the lips of Christ (Mt 6:14–15). We most perfectly resemble our heavenly Father and the Lord Jesus when we forgive those who wrong us (Mt 5:43–48; Lk 23:34). It is not a suggestion but an absolute prerequisite to enjoying eternal life.

So long as we are in the body we must be on guard against succumbing to sin. Mortal sin is a terrifying possibility, but it goes hand-in-hand with our having been endowed with free will. God desires children, not robots; and that means that, aided by grace, we must choose to love him by obeying his commands. Our justification is ongoing; his power enables us to conquer temptation and to progress in virtue.

FINAL JUSTIFICATION

Our final justification comes only when we stand before Christ the judge. James tells us, "Be patient, therefore, brethren, until the coming of the Lord. Behold, the farmer waits for the precious fruit of the earth, being patient over it until it receives the early and the late rain. You also be patient. Establish your hearts, for the coming of the Lord is at hand" (5:7–8). It is then that the imperishable seed of which we were born finally blossoms into a heavenly life. St. Paul tells us that our finite minds cannot conceive of the future that awaits us, although the Spirit does give intimations (1 Cor 2:9–10). John wrote, "Beloved, we are God's children now; it does not yet appear what we shall be, but we know that when [Christ] appears *we shall be like him*, for we shall see him as he is" (1 Jn 3:2).[33] But Paul offered a caveat: "we are children of God, and if children, then heirs, heirs of God and fellow heirs with Christ, *provided we suffer with him* in order that we may also be glorified with him" (Rom 8:16–17).

Jesus said that the days before his return would be the most tumultuous in history. "[B]ecause wickedness is multiplied, most men's love will grow cold. But he who endures to the end will be saved" (Mt 24:12–13). He also told us what we must do to persevere: "watch at all times, *praying that you may have the strength to escape* all these things that will take place, and stand before the Son of man" (Luke 21:36).[34] Ultimately, we ask to participate in Jesus's own perseverance, his obedient love in the face of death.

---

33 If we die in God's friendship but still lacking the holiness required to fully participate in the life of heaven, the Lord provides the needed purification, or what the Church calls *purgatory*. For a scriptural explanation see Kapler, *Hebrews*, 96–99.
34 "... with regard to the gift of perseverance, of which it is written: He that shall persevere to the end, he shall be saved [Mt 10:22; 24:13], which cannot be obtained from anyone except from Him who is able to make him stand who stands [Rom 14:4], that he may stand perseveringly, and to raise him who falls, let no one promise himself herein something as certain with an absolute certainty, though all ought to place and repose the firmest hope in God's help. For God, unless men themselves fail in His grace, as he has begun a good work, so will he perfect it, working to will and to accomplish [Phil 1:6; 2:13]." Council of Trent, *Decree on Justification*, 13.

I keep that in mind when I read James's call that we petition God for wisdom (1:5), a "wisdom from above" that is "first pure, then peaceable, gentle, open to reason, full of mercy and good fruits, without uncertainty or insincerity" (3:17). God wishes to give this wisdom to all, "generously and without reproaching" (1:5). I believe this to be the wisdom of the Cross, of Christ crucified (1 Cor 1:23–24). This wisdom is God's gift, a synergy of faith and works, through which Christ manifests his paschal mystery before the world.

CHAPTER 4

The Redemptive Nature of Suffering

"Blessed is the man who endures trial..."

James 1:12

IT IS ONE OF THE MOST DIFFICULT SUBJECTS we can broach—suffering. It is part of the great mystery of why God tolerates evil. Theists of every stripe have struggled to answer "Why?" The Christian believes that God, rather than answer by way of an inspired treatise, did the unimaginable: He became one of us and suffered torture and death to obtain our salvation. God, in a sense, bypassed the explanation—which he indicated we could not, at this time, understand (Job 38:1–18)—and instead took our experience of suffering onto himself. And in that incarnational embrace, he makes it possible for suffering to have a role in our attainment of final salvation. Large swathes of Christianity no longer proclaim this element of the gospel; but with James as our guide, we want to open ourselves to the wisdom of the Cross and recognize the full extent of Christ's redemptive action.

JAMES ON THE VALUE OF SUFFERING TRIALS

James places this revolutionary element of the gospel right at the beginning of his letter. "Count it all joy, my brethren, when you meet various trials, for you know that the testing of your faith produces steadfastness. And let steadfastness have its full effect, that you may be perfect and complete, lacking in nothing" (1:2–4).

James speaks of "various trials" that test our faith. We might assume that he refers specifically to religious trials, acts of discrimination or violence perpetrated against us because of our faith in Christ. Protestant biblical scholar Douglas J. Moo understands James to cast his net much wider, though, referring to the full gambit of trials that test our faith in God's love, goodness, and justice: betrayal, sickness, loneliness, bereavement, poverty.[1] James finds himself in agreement with Paul on this point (2 Cor 12:9–10;

---

1   Moo, *James*, 54; cf. Johnson, *James*, 157.

Phil 4:11–13). James wanted his readers to understand that difficulties are part of every disciple's life. The wisdom literature from which he drew was adamant on this point:

> My child, when you come to serve the Lord, prepare yourself for trials. Be sincere of heart and steadfast, and do not be impetuous in time of adversity. Cling to him, do not leave him, that you may prosper in your last days. Accept whatever happens to you; in periods of humiliation be patient. For in fire gold is tested, and the chosen, in the crucible of humiliation. (Sirach 2:1–5, NABRE)

The word that James selected for "testing," *dokiminion*, is a rare Greek verb that occurs only twice in the Septuagint, Proverbs 27:21 and Psalm 11:7,[2] where it refers to the refining of silver and gold.[3]

What is revolutionary in James's statement is the idea that Christians should look upon trials as occasions for intense joy. The Greek text helps us understand his rationale. "Joy" is *charan*, from the root word *charis*, or "grace." Christians are able to recognize trials as occasions for joy precisely because God's grace is at work to bring them successfully through the period of testing and perfect the image of Christ within their souls.

We image Christ precisely in his Passion. When James says that the testing of our faith produces "steadfastness," or "endurance," he uses the Greek term *hypomonēn*. Etymologically, it points to "remaining under" a heavy load. For the Christian this load is Christ's *Cross* that we must carry as did the Master (Mt 16:24) if we are to become "perfect and complete, lacking in nothing" (Jas 1:4).

Paul and Peter were of the same mind as James:

ROMANS 5:3–5	1 PETER 1:6–7
... we rejoice [*kauchaomai*—glory, boast] in our sufferings, knowing that suffering produces endurance [*hypomonēn*], and endurance produces character, and character produces hope, and hope does not disappoint us, because God's love has been poured into our hearts through the Holy Spirit who has been given to us.	In this you rejoice, though now for a little while you may have to suffer various trials, so that the genuineness of your faith, more precious than gold which though perishable is tested [*dokiminion*] by fire, may redound to praise and glory and honor at the revelation of Jesus Christ.

---

2   Ps 12:6 in modern translations.
3   Moo, *James*, 58.

The apostles knew that it was one thing to act Christlike when life proceeds smoothly, but quite another to display Christ's character and virtues in the fire of trials. They are the "resistance training" of the spiritual life. Peter went so far as to counsel the *enslaved* among his flock that, "one is approved if, mindful of God, he endures pain while suffering unjustly.... *For to this you have been called*, because Christ also suffered for you, leaving you an example that you should follow in his steps" (1 Pet 2:19–21).

We Christians are not masochists. We do not embrace suffering as an end in itself. Rather, through it, we embrace our crucified Lord, so as to arrive with him at the glory of the Resurrection. James continues, "Blessed is the man who endures trial, for when he has stood the test he will receive the crown of life which God has promised to those who love him" (1:12). We find ourselves in the same position as Jesus who, "for the joy that was set before him endured the cross, despising the shame, and is [now] seated at the right hand of the throne of God" (Heb 12:2). When we persist in faith in the Father's love for us, committing our lives into his hands despite the pain we endure, it is then that we *most resemble* the Lord Jesus—*and that is what makes our suffering redemptive.*

God allows us to pass through testing with that positive end in view. James does offer a word of caution, though. As beneficial as these periods of trial are for our souls, they are also when we find ourselves most susceptible to temptation (1:12–15). The temptation comes not from God, but from concupiscence. Our disordered appetites act like a siren song calling us to seek relief and distraction in activities at odds with God's will—whether that be lashing out in anger, drowning our sorrows in a bottle, illicit sexual pleasure, or denying the faith in order to escape persecution. The devil, always the opportunist, seeks to capitalize on our areas of weakness.

If grace is the means for recognizing trials as occasions for joy, then grace is also the means by which we can escape temptation and persevere under the weight of the cross. How do we increase the flow of God's grace? James has the answer: "Is any one among you suffering? *Let him pray*" (5:13). Jesus seems to have crafted the final two petitions of the Our Father for just such moments: "And lead us not into temptation, but deliver us from evil" (Mt 6:13).

We should feel no guilt about asking the Lord to deliver us from suffering. Suffering is, in and of itself, an experience of evil; we are being deprived of a good that, in the normal order of things, "ought" to be ours.[4] It is only natural for men and women to seek freedom from their sufferings, just as Jesus did in the Garden of Gethsemane. The Lord fell to the ground three times and through loud cries and tears petitioned the Father that, if possible, he be spared the cup of suffering (Mt 26:44; Heb 5:7). Instead of relief, an angel was sent to strengthen him for what lay ahead (Lk 22:43). Scripture tells us that this was for a great purpose; the Epistle to the Hebrews goes so far as to say that Jesus was "made perfect" by his obedient acceptance of suffering (Heb 5:8–9). It was *the means* by which his humanity was "perfected" (*teleioō* in Greek, "completed," or "brought to fullness"). The "indestructible life" of the Resurrection was obtained by way of the Cross (Heb 7:16).

The Apostle Paul shared an experience strikingly similar to that of our Lord Jesus. Paul suffered a humiliating "thorn in the flesh," possibly a physical ailment (2 Cor 12:7). While Paul recognized its positive effect of keeping him from becoming puffed up, he nonetheless petitioned the Lord three times to have the thorn removed. Rather than grant his request, the Lord responded, "My grace is sufficient for you, for my power is made perfect in weakness," leading Paul to proclaim, "I will all the more gladly boast of my weaknesses, that the power of Christ may rest upon me. For the sake of Christ, then, I am content with weaknesses, insults, hardships, persecutions, and calamities; for when I am weak, then I am strong" (2 Cor 12:9–10).[5] Just as Jesus submitted to the Father's will that the *world's salvation* be obtained through his suffering, so Paul submitted to the Father's will that his *personal salvation* be furthered by the same means. The

---

4 John Paul II, *Salvifici Doloris*, 7, https://w2.vatican.va/content/john-paul-ii/en/apost_letters/1984/documents/hf_jp-ii_apl_11021984_salvifici-doloris.html.

5 Note how, like James, Paul sees any form of suffering as potentially redemptive—so long as it is borne in faith. Paul's "thorn in the flesh" was far from his only suffering. Earlier in 2 Corinthians he recounted, "Five times I have received at the hands of the Jews the forty lashes less one. Three times I have been beaten with rods; once I was stoned. Three times I have been shipwrecked; a night and a day I have been adrift at sea; on frequent journeys, in danger from rivers, danger from robbers, danger from my own people, danger from Gentiles, danger in the city, danger in the wilderness, danger at sea, danger from false brethren; in toil and hardship, through many a sleepless night, in hunger and thirst, often without food, in cold and exposure. And, apart from other things, there is the daily pressure upon me of my anxiety for all the churches" (2 Cor 11:24–28).

heart of Jesus's prayer in Gethsemane was "not as I will, [Father,] but as thou wilt" (Mt 26:39); and he intends the same for us. "Pray like *this*: Our Father... Thy will be done, on earth as it is in heaven" (Mt 6:9–10). As James told us above, it is through steadfastness in trials that we, like Jesus, become *teleioō*, or "perfect" (1:4).

THE RESURRECTION AND THE EXAMPLE OF JOB

James returns to the theme of steadfastness towards the conclusion of the epistle:

> Be patient, therefore, brethren, until the coming of the Lord. Behold, the farmer waits for the precious fruit of the earth, being patient over it until it receives the early and the late rain. You also be patient. Establish your hearts, for the coming of the Lord is at hand.... As an example of suffering and patience, brethren, take the prophets who spoke in the name of the Lord. Behold, we call those happy who were steadfast. You have heard of the steadfastness of Job, and you have seen the purpose of the Lord, how the Lord is compassionate and merciful. (James 5:7–11)

The Second Coming is the definitive answer to our trials and sufferings. Christ will "wipe every tear from [our] eyes, and death shall be no more" (Rev 21:4). If we see that Day delayed, it is only because of God's mercy.[6] James writes of the early rains (October to November) that cause the seed to germinate, and the late rains (April to May) necessary to mature the crop.[7] God wants to give us

---

6 "The Lord is not slow about his promise as some count slowness, *but is forbearing toward you, not wishing that any should perish, but that all should reach repentance*. But the day of the Lord will come like a thief, and then the heavens will pass away with a loud noise, and the elements will be dissolved with fire, and the earth and the works that are upon it will be burned up. Since all these things are thus to be dissolved, what sort of persons ought you to be in lives of holiness and godliness, waiting for and hastening the coming of the day of God, because of which the heavens will be kindled and dissolved, and the elements will melt with fire! But according to his promise we wait for new heavens and a new earth in which righteousness dwells. Therefore, beloved, since you wait for these, be zealous to be found by him without spot or blemish, and at peace. And *count the forbearance of our Lord as salvation*" (2 Peter 3:9–14).

7 Martin, *James*, 249.

every opportunity to grow in grace before the time of harvesting. The "implanted word" James spoke of at the beginning of his letter must be given every opportunity to reach maturity. Sometimes we must weather a brutal storm to receive the abundant, nourishing waters of the Spirit. Eventually, the storm is no more and we behold only the magnificent plant that drank up the falling rain. That will be us, glorified in body and soul when Christ returns.

James did not traffic in pious platitudes. It is impossible to exaggerate how radically Christ's Resurrection altered James's and the other apostles' understanding of suffering. On Easter Sunday, they saw the same Jesus who only days earlier had been placed in a tomb, his body one great wound, now standing before them completely victorious over the evil he had endured. The wounds in his hands, feet, and side were now like glorious medals proclaiming his infinite love for the Father and mankind. Christ was not merely resuscitated but *raised to a completely new manner of life,* a glimpse and foretaste of the new creation promised to the disciples!

We see the effect that Jesus's Resurrection, and the coming of the Spirit, had upon the apostles. When Jesus was condemned by the Sanhedrin and handed over to Pilate, all but John fled in fear for their lives. Then, within a matter of months, the Twelve became so outspoken that, when beaten by the Sanhedrin and ordered never to speak of Jesus again, they went away, "rejoicing that they were counted worthy to suffer dishonor for the name. And every day in the temple and at home they did not cease teaching and preaching Jesus as the Christ" (Acts 5:41–42). Death had been robbed of its finality. The pain of beating, real as it was, was rescued from meaninglessness because it conformed the apostles to the image of Christ. The Father did not intervene to stop the Sanhedrin from perpetrating an evil act, but in an act of divine alchemy, transformed it into an opportunity for the apostles to experience Christ dying and rising *in them.*[8]

---

8 As St. Paul later wrote, "But we have this treasure in earthen vessels, to show that the transcendent power belongs to God and not to us. We are afflicted in every way, but not crushed; perplexed, but not driven to despair; persecuted, but not forsaken; struck down, but not destroyed; *always carrying in the body the death of Jesus, so that the life of Jesus may also be manifested in our bodies.* For while we live we are always being given up to death for Jesus's sake, so that the life of Jesus may be manifested in our mortal flesh" (2 Cor 4:7–11).

In this same vein, Peter wrote, "Beloved, do not be surprised at the fiery ordeal which comes upon you to prove you, as though something strange were

We will see this on a global scale as history reaches its climax. *The Catechism of the Catholic Church* (675–77) summarizes the scriptural data for us:

> Before Christ's second coming the Church must pass through a final trial that will shake the faith of many believers [Lk 18:8; Mt 24:12]. The persecution that accompanies her pilgrimage on earth [Lk 21:12; Jn 15:19–20] will unveil the "mystery of iniquity" in the form of a religious deception offering men an apparent solution to their problems at the price of apostasy from the truth.... The Church will enter the glory of the kingdom only through this final Passover, when she will follow the Lord in his death and Resurrection [Rev 19:1–9].[9]

Prior to this final Passover, our lives are a tension between periodic experiences of the Cross and foretastes of the Resurrection. We observe this pattern throughout the Acts of the Apostles, with its intertwining stories of persecution and miracles. We also find it in the gospels: Jesus miraculously fed the hungry, healed all manner of illness, cast out devils, and raised the dead, while simultaneously declaring "blessed" those who were poor, mourning, reviled and persecuted![10]

In the last chapter, we saw James adamant that it was Abraham's *response to testing* that brought his faith to completion (2:22). Abraham was able to place his son upon the wood of sacrifice — in effect,

---

happening to you. But rejoice in so far *as you share Christ's sufferings*, that you may also rejoice and be glad when his glory is revealed. If you are reproached for the name of Christ, you are blessed, because the spirit of glory and of God rests upon you.... If one suffers as a Christian, let him not be ashamed, but under that name let him glorify God. For the time has come for judgment to begin with the household of God; and if it begins with us, what will be the end of those who do not obey the gospel of God?... Therefore let those who suffer according to God's will do right and entrust their souls to a faithful Creator" (1 Pet 4:12–14, 16–17, 19).

9 Belief in the "rapture," first proposed at the end of the nineteenth century and popularized in the second half of the twentieth, is part of the larger movement in Western Christianity to deny suffering's place in the Christian life. There are a number of effective, scriptural responses to proponents of the rapture; as a summary I humbly offer my own treatment in *The God Who is Love: Explaining Christianity From Its Center* (St. Louis: Out of the Box, 2009), 139–41.
10 John Paul II, *Salvifici Doloris*, 15.

join himself to the Cross—because faith allowed him to grasp that his God could raise the dead (Heb 11:19). The manner in which we endure our trials—committing ourselves, via the movement of grace, into the Father's hands with our eyes fixed on the resurrection—is an important way that our faith is manifested in deeds.

As additional examples of how we are to react to suffering, James tells us to "take the prophets who spoke in the name of the Lord. Behold, we call those happy who were steadfast. You have heard of the steadfastness [*hypomonēn*] of Job, and you have seen the purpose of the Lord, how the Lord is compassionate and merciful" (5:10–11). With Job, James enlists the help of the OT's ultimate example of faithfulness in time of trial. In the story, Job was said to be the most upright man on earth. And yet, God allowed Satan to afflict him—the death of his children, financial ruin, sickness, and the misunderstanding and condemnation of his wife and friends. Despite all of his suffering, Job refused to curse the Lord. Instead, from the midst of his agony, he expressed a mysterious hope in the resurrection.[11] Because of his faithfulness, God returned to Job double all that he had lost.

Even in outline form, the story is an encouragement; but the Book of Job has much more to teach us. When we delve into it, we find that Job's faithfulness did not preclude him undertaking an agonizing theological quest to understand why God allowed him to suffer. The bulk of the book is an argument between Job and his three closest friends. They insisted that Job's suffering was a punishment for sin, while he maintained his innocence. It was not that Job's friends were wrong in principle; from the earliest strata of the Old Testament forward, suffering is recognized as a corrective punishment for sin.[12] The greatest articulation of the principle is probably Hebrews 12:5–13.[13] Job knew that this wasn't

---

11   "For I know that my Redeemer lives, and at last he will stand upon the earth; and after my skin has been thus destroyed, then from my flesh I shall see God, whom I shall see on my side, and my eyes shall behold, and not another" (Job 19:25–27).

12   E.g., Gen 3:16–20; Ex 7:14–18; Ex 9:1–4; Deut 4:25–32; 2 Sam 7:14; Jer 6:11–12; 2 Macc 6:12–13; Rom 2:2; 1 Cor 11:29–32.

13   "Have you forgotten the exhortation which addresses you as sons?—'My son, do not regard lightly the discipline of the Lord, nor lose courage when you are punished by him. For the Lord disciplines him whom he loves, and chastises every son whom he receives' [Prov 3:11–12]. It is for discipline that you have to

true in his case, though, and demanded that God explain why an innocent, like himself, suffers.

God did finally respond, and from the midst of a whirlwind, no less. He denied Job's attempt to put him on trial, reminding him who was the Creator and who was but a creature:

> Who is this that darkens counsel by words without knowledge? Gird up your loins like a man, I will question you, and you shall declare to me. Where were you when I laid the foundation of the earth? Tell me, if you have understanding. Who determined its measurements—surely you know!... Have you entered into the springs of the sea, or walked in the recesses of the deep?... Declare, if you know all this. (Job 38:2–5, 16, 18)

If Job could not understand the mysteries of creation, then how would he ever understand a mystery as sublime as why God allows the innocent to suffer? Job did find peace—even before God restored his family, material goods, and his health. *God's revelation, his drawing near, quelled Job's anguish.* "I had heard of thee [Lord] by the hearing of the ear, but now my eye sees thee; therefore I despise myself, and repent in dust and ashes" (42:5–6). Job no longer flailed blindly, as if God had abandoned him to the darkness. The Lord was near, asking Job to let go of his need to understand why, and simply surrender himself into his strong hand. To know, by faith, that God is present in the midst of pain, can communicate a supernatural peace. It is beyond human comprehension (Phil 4:7).

God revealed himself to Job in the theophany of the whirlwind; but he revealed himself to James and the apostles as the Incarnate Word, the source of supernatural joy in the midst of suffering. In Jesus, the Almighty "took sin upon himself and atoned for it. He also took suffering upon himself and sanctified it."[14] Jesus draws

---

endure. God is treating you as sons; for what son is there whom his father does not discipline? If you are left without discipline, in which all have participated, then you are illegitimate children and not sons.... For the moment all discipline seems painful rather than pleasant; later it yields the peaceful fruit of righteousness to those who have been trained by it. Therefore lift your drooping hands and strengthen your weak knees, and make straight paths for your feet, so that what is lame may not be put out of joint but rather be healed" (Heb 12:5–8, 11–13).

14 Hubert van Zeller, *The Mystery of Suffering* (Notre Dame: Christian Classics, 2015), 9.

near to us in the Eucharist, Scripture, personal prayer, and our fellow Christians—*as near to us as he was to James and the Twelve.*

You and I, like Job, may rarely understand why God allows our trials and sufferings, what specific good he intends for them to accomplish. On occasion, we may recognize his fatherly correction—he may require a penance over and above the one assigned in the confessional to undo the damage our sins cause ourselves and others. (Recall Peter's painful experience in John 21:15–17, when, to heal his soul of the effects of his threefold denial, Christ requested a threefold profession of love.[15]) At other times, God may allow us to suffer so he can miraculously intervene as testimony to the faith (see Jn 9:3). Most of the time we will remain in the dark regarding God's specific purpose in allowing a trial. In each of our hardships, even as we pray for relief, we are meant to join ourselves to Christ and commit the outcome into the Father's hands.

When we pray in this way, our souls are flooded with the grace to endure the Cross and progress incrementally forward toward the Resurrection. On that Day, all our questions about suffering will be answered. "Now I know in part; then I shall understand fully, even as I have been fully understood" (1 Cor 13:12). Until then, we say with St. Paul and Job, "[I]n any and all circumstances I have learned the secret of facing plenty and hunger, abundance and want. I can do all things in him who strengthens me" (Phil 4:12–13); "the LORD gave, and the LORD has taken away; blessed be the name of the LORD" (Job 1:21).

OUR SUFFERINGS BENEFIT OTHERS

James has helped us establish a foundational Christian understanding of suffering, one we are now in a position to build upon. Saint Paul reveals another element of the mystery: Not only can suffering be redemptive for us personally, but the grace we receive at such moments *spills over to other members of Christ's mystical body.* Many Christians are unacquainted with this belief, but it is grounded in Scripture and Tradition.

---

[15] Saint Paul also taught the Corinthians that some of their number had become weak, ill, and even died because they partook of the Eucharist in an unworthy manner. He explained that "when we are judged by the Lord, we are chastened so that we may not be condemned along with the world" (1 Cor 11:30–32). These punishments were meant to evoke repentance.

The *locus classicus* for the teaching is Colossians 1:24. From prison Paul wrote, "Now I rejoice in my sufferings *for your sake*, and in *my flesh* I complete what is *lacking* in Christ's afflictions for the sake of his body, that is, the Church" (Col. 1:24). First, let us be clear that Paul was not placing a limit on the redemptive scope of Christ's Passion. From everything else he wrote, we know that Paul held Jesus's sacrifice to be absolutely sufficient. Christ, *and he alone*, has redeemed us from the guilt of our sins and united us to the Father. Second, we have also seen Paul's conviction that we must suffer with Christ if we are to be raised with him (Rom 8:16–17) and that it is in times of suffering that Christ imparts additional grace to the soul and advances us toward final justification (2 Cor 12:9; Phil 3:10–12; Acts 14:22). These two truths harmonize to explain how Paul's sufferings could benefit the Colossians.

I suggest the following synthesis: Christ's obedience in suffering paid the eternal debt of sin and won redemption for the human race. United to him, the sufferings of his Church are a divinely ordained means for *appropriating* the grace of redemption. Grace descends not just upon the individual bearing his or her suffering, but upon other Christians. That is what Paul communicated, in a shorthand way, when he told the Colossians that he rejoiced in the sufferings he underwent for *their* sake. The benefit that Paul's sufferings afforded the Colossians could not have been earthly blessings. The cell from which he wrote to them was most likely in Rome, 1,200 miles away. Paul had never visited the Colossians, nor had he any hand in evangelizing them (1:4; 2:1). If the Colossians reaped some benefit from Paul's suffering, it was a *spiritual* benefit. This is but another facet of Paul's well-known teaching that Christ and the Church form one mystical person, wherein each member enriches the others (1 Cor 12:12–27; Eph 4:11–16).

Allow me to go a bit more in depth into the points just considered. I want to stress that it was the sufferings *of Christ*, the head of the mystical body, which merited salvation for the human race:

> [H]e was wounded for our transgressions, he was bruised for our iniquities; upon him was the chastisement that made us whole, and with his stripes we are healed ... the Lord has laid on him the iniquity of us all.... [I]t was

the will of the LORD to bruise him.... [H]e bore the
sin of many, and made intercession for the transgressors.
(Is 53:5–6, 10a, 12b)

Jesus is the redeemer, and baptism unites us to him. He lives in us, and we live in him. This makes it possible for our sufferings to be drawn into his and offered to the Father. It is a mystery analogous to that of the Eucharist: Christ presents *us* to the Father, "This is *my Body*, this is my Blood."[16] If Christ's obedience while suffering the Passion merited the redemption of our race, then his suffering *in us*—the trustful surrender to the Father that he produces in our souls—can merit the application of redemptive graces to our brothers and sisters.[17] The Redeemer *makes the sufferings of his members* redemptive.

This teaching in no way denies Christ's position as the sole mediator between God and man. As members of his body, we Christians intercede from "within" him (1 Tim 2:1–5). The thought that we play a role in others' salvation may seem scandalous to some, but it is thoroughly biblical. Did not God make the world's salvation dependent upon the preaching of the apostles? They extended Christ's teaching ministry beyond the borders of Israel: "we are ambassadors for Christ, God making his appeal *through us*" (2 Cor 5:20; cf. Rom 10:14; 1 Tim 4:16; Jude 22–23). If the Church can participate in this aspect of Christ's redeeming work, then why not his work of suffering?

The Passion narratives indicate that we can. "As they led [Jesus] away, they seized one Simon of Cyrene, who was coming in from the country, and laid on him the cross, to carry it behind Jesus" (Lk 23:26;

---

16 Early in his epistle, James calls Christians "a kind of firstfruits of [God's] creatures" (1:18). It is cultic language—a reference to *Bikkurim*, the Feast of the First Fruits, when Israelites brought the first sheaves of the harvest to the Temple. The priest accepted them and placed them before the altar as he offered a *lamb*, cake of *bread*, and *wine* in sacrifice to the Lord (Lev 23:9–14; Deut 26:1–4). It is another striking image of the way Christ joins us to his sacrifice, made present at each Eucharist. My sincere thanks to Phillip Kapler for making this important connection for me.

17 Consider how Luke narrates the martyrdom of Stephen in terms of Christ's crucifixion (Lk 23:34, 46; Acts 7:58–8:1), and how Stephen's prayer bore fruit in the conversion of Paul. Jesus's first words to the future apostle cemented, in Paul's mind, this identification between the sufferings of the Church and those of Christ: "Saul, Saul, why do you persecute *me*?" (Acts 9:4–5).

Mt 27:32; Mk 15:21). Scourged and beaten, Jesus needed Simon's help to make it to the top of Golgotha to complete His sacrifice. Simon lifted the heavy, blood-smeared beam onto his own shoulders and followed after Jesus. Even though all the value and power of the sacrifice flowed from Christ, Simon truly shared a part of the Lord's Passion. It was not Simon who redeemed the world, but his pain and exertion while carrying the cross assisted Jesus to make his offering. Objectively speaking, Simon cooperated in Christ's redemptive act.[18]

What is true of Simon in a purely physical sense is true of the Blessed Virgin Mary in a comprehensive sense. When Mary presented Jesus in the Temple, the elderly Simeon prophesied: "this child is set for the fall and the rising of many in Israel, and for a sign that is spoken against (and a sword will pierce through your own soul *also*) that thoughts out of many hearts may be revealed" (Lk 2:34–35). United to Christ, but obviously subordinate to him, Mary's suffering bore fruit in the application of grace to souls!

The sword that pierced her heart, *rhomphaia* in Greek, was not the short sword of the Romans but the long, broad sword of the Thracians. Three decades later, gazing up at her crucified Son, Mary's soul suffered each wound, bore each insult that Jesus did. Just as the Cross cast its shadow backward over Jesus's entire life, so too Mary's: she gave birth to Jesus in a stable, fled with him for their lives into Egypt, suffered three days of anguish when Jesus was lost in the Temple, not to mention the untold, daily struggles of first-century life. Mary experienced and shared Jesus's earthly sufferings more completely and intensely than anyone. (The very flesh and blood with which Jesus redeemed the world were taken from her!)

Each Christian is meant to replicate the experiences of Mary and Simon. In baptism, we become Christ's flesh and blood. Like an extension of the Incarnation, Jesus clothes himself in our persons and lifts our sufferings up into his eternal offering to the Father (Heb 9:14). Left to ourselves, we would never choose the Cross; but it is laid upon our shoulders. Like Simon, we are pressed into service—the loss of a job, illness, abandonment by a spouse. We struggle under its weight, trying our best to remedy what has gone wrong; but like Mary at the Annunciation and Christ in

---

[18] But make no mistake—Simon's ability to cooperate remained completely dependent upon Christ, who in his divine nature *held Simon in existence*.

Gethsemane we pray, "let it be to me according to your word" (Lk 1:38). We make this prayer by grace, and God responds by sending more grace—grace for us, grace for brothers and sisters we may never meet here on earth—so we can bear the Cross and arrive at the glory of the Resurrection.

In suffering, Jesus draws us more deeply into his own priestly ministry. Under the New Covenant, Jesus is both priest and victim. As members of his body, by extension, the same can be said of us. Saint Peter calls us a "kingdom of priests," and counsels, "let yourselves be built into a spiritual house to be a holy priesthood to offer spiritual sacrifices acceptable to God through Jesus Christ" (1 Pet 2:9, 5, NABRE); Paul goes on to say that our "spiritual worship" consists in "presenting [our] bodies as living sacrifices" (Rom 12:1). United to Christ, we are both priests and victims.

Do you recall from the previous section the Epistle to the Hebrews' claim that Jesus was made "perfect" (*teleioō*) through suffering? There is a second layer of meaning. You see, when an Israelite was ordained to the priesthood, his hands were anointed with oil. In the Greek translation of the OT, *teleioō* was used in place of the Hebrew idiom, "fill up the hands" (Ex 29:29, 35; Lev 8:33; 16:32; 21:10; Num 3:3).[19] With this in mind, Hebrews 5:8–9 takes on added significance, "[Jesus] learned obedience through what he suffered; and *being made perfect* [*teleioō*] he became the source of eternal salvation to all who obey him, being *designated by God a high priest* according to the order of Melchizedek" (Heb 5:8–10). Jesus was consecrated to the priesthood via obedience in the midst of suffering! Hebrews applies the same term, *teleioō*, to the spirits of the just in heaven (Heb 12:24)—the same spirits the Book of Revelation shows participating in Christ's *priestly* intercession before the Father's throne (Rev 5:8; Heb 7:25).[20]

For those of us still on earth, we understand this to mean that Christ unites our earthly sufferings to his and transmutes them into spiritual sacrifices. Further, we recognize that the Father accepts such sacrifices and reciprocates with unmatched generosity: "Give, and it will be given to you; good measure, pressed down, shaken together and running over, will be put into your lap" (Lk 6:38).

---

19 Kapler, *Hebrews*, 35.
20 Ibid., 93.

All of this explains why Paul could rejoice in his suffering: it was a priestly offering, supernaturally valuable, and beneficial for his brothers and sisters.

THE POST-APOSTOLIC CHURCH'S UNDERSTANDING OF SUFFERING

The redemptive value that the apostles recognized in suffering continued to be faithfully communicated by their successors. Ignatius, the Bishop of Antioch, Syria, wrote of suffering and martyrdom during his transport to Rome, on his way to die in the Colosseum (AD 110). Many of Ignatius's statements echo Paul's teaching on suffering. In Ignatius's *Epistle to the Ephesians* he wrote, "My spirit is in sacrificial service for the cross, which is a scandal to unbelievers [1 Cor 1:18]"; and he told the Magnesians, "If we do not willingly embrace dying for his passion, neither is his life in us [Rom 8:17]." When Ignatius wrote to the Christians in Rome, he asked that they not attempt to intervene on his behalf: "Permit me to be an imitator of the sufferings of my God. If anyone possesses [Christ] in himself, let him consider what I want and let him suffer with me."[21] Like Paul, he saw his life being poured out as a "libation," a drink offering.[22] He linked his martyrdom to the offering of Christ, re-presented to the Father in the Church's Eucharist: "Permit me to be food for the beasts, through them I will reach God. I am the wheat of God and I compete through beasts' teeth to be found the pure bread of Christ."[23]

Ignatius's sacrifice consisted of more than the act of martyrdom. It had already begun in the mistreatment he suffered at the hands of his Roman captors (Rom 5:1). Kenneth Howell, in his masterful new translation and commentary on Ignatius's epistles, highlights the bishop's use of *antipsuchon*, or "substitute soul." Appropriating Paul's words to the Colossians, Ignatius knew that his suffering benefited more souls than just his own.[24] He told the Smyrneans:

---

[21] Ignatius of Antioch, *Epistle to the Romans*, 6:3, in Kenneth Howell, *Ignatius of Antioch and Polycarp of Smyrna: A New Translation and Theological Commentary* (Zanesville, OH: CHResources, 2009), 116–17.

[22] *Epistle to the Romans*, 2:2; *Epistle to the Philadelphians* 5:1; Phil 2:17; 2 Tim 4:6.

[23] *Epistle to the Romans*, 4:4, Howell, 114.

[24] Kenneth Howell, *Ignatius of Antioch*, 14.

"My spirit and my bonds are your substitute soul";[25] and their bishop Polycarp, "I and my bonds that you love are your substitute soul in every way."[26] To the Trallians he wrote, "My spirit makes you pure *not only now* but also when I attain to God."[27] He expounded upon Paul's theology of the mystical body in his letter to the Philadelphians:

> My brothers, I am being completely poured out for love of you and with exceeding joy *I try to make you secure*. It is really not I *but Jesus Christ* who does so. In him, as a prisoner I am all the more afraid because I am still incomplete. However, *your prayer will make me complete* for God so that I may obtain a share in the lot where I received mercy.[28]

Ignatius made it clear that it was *Christ* who accomplished all of this *in his body*. Union with Christ would make the Philadelphians' prayer for Ignatius efficacious and his perseverance in suffering meritorious for them.

The early Church knew that God's providence extended to every area of their lives. The *Didache*, or *The Teaching of the Twelve Apostles* (c. AD 100), directed readers to "accept as blessings the casualties that befall you, assured that nothing happens without God."[29] Cyprian of Carthage (d. 258) taught that God made use of calamity to correct the erring; but he also recognized some sufferings as no more than the consequence of life in a fallen world: "[W]e are all, good and evil, contained in one household. Whatever happens within the house we suffer with equal fate, until, when the end of the temporal life shall be attained, we shall be distributed among the homes either of eternal death or immortality."[30] It is our union with Christ that injects meaning and purpose into these common sufferings.

---

25 *Epistle to the Smyrneans*, 10:2, Howell, 135.
26 *Epistle to Polycarp*, 2:3, Howell, 141.
27 *Epistle to the Trallians*, 13:3, Howell, 109–10.
28 *Epistle to the Philadelphians*, 5:1, Howell, 124.
29 Johannes Quasten, ed., *The Didache, The Epistle of Barnabus, the Epistles and the Martyrdom of St. Polycarp, the Fragments of Papias, the Epistle to Diognetus*, Ancient Christian Writers, trans. James A. Kleist (New York: Paulist Press, 1948).
30 Cyprian of Carthage, *To Demetrianus*, Treatise 5.19; quoted in Leo D. Lefebure, "The Understanding of Suffering in the Early Church," *CLARITAS Journal of Dialogue and Culture* 4.2 (October 2015), 33.

The Church's meditation upon suffering has continued down through the centuries. In the thirteenth century, for instance, St. Anthony of Padua sagely remarked, "God sends us afflictions for various reasons: first, to increase our merit; second, to preserve in us the grace of God; third, to punish us for our sins; and fourth, to show forth his glory and his other attributes." Thomas à Kempis, in his fifteenth-century *The Imitation of Christ*, wrote:

> If there had been anything better for men, more profitable for their salvation, than suffering, you may be sure that Christ, by his teaching and his own example, would have pointed it out. But no: addressing the disciples who were following him, and all those who wish to follow him, he clearly urges them to carry the cross, when he says, *If any man has a mind to come my way, let him renounce himself, and take up his cross, and follow me* [Lk 9:23]. So then, when we have made an end of reading and studying, this is the conclusion we should reach at last: *that we cannot enter the kingdom of heaven without many trials* [Acts 14:22].[31]

In our own time, Pope St. John Paul II reflected deeply upon the subject in his apostolic letter *Savifici Doloris*, or *On the Christian Meaning of Human Suffering*. John Paul, the man with a ready smile and an almost perpetual twinkle in the eye, was nonetheless intimately acquainted with suffering. His mother died when he was only eight years old, and his father and brother before he turned twenty-one. He lived decades of his life under Nazi and Soviet occupation. He survived an assassin's bullet and endured the debilitating effects of Parkinson's disease. John Paul descended into some of the darkest experiential places known to man, only to discover that he was not alone; the Crucified was there, awaiting him.

> Christ does not explain in the abstract the reason for suffering, but before all else he says:
> "Follow me! Come! Take part through your suffering in this work of saving the world, a salvation achieved through my suffering! Through my cross." Gradually,

---

[31] Thomas à Kempis, *The Imitation of Christ*, trans. Ronald Knox and Michael Oakley (San Francisco: Ignatius Press, 2005), Book 2, 12:15, 103–4.

as the individual takes up his cross, spiritually uniting himself to the cross of Christ, the salvific meaning of suffering is revealed before him. He does not discover this meaning at his own human level, but at the level of the sufferings of Christ. At the same time, however, from this level of Christ the salvific meaning of suffering *descends to man's level* and becomes, in a sense, the individual's personal response. It is then that man finds in his suffering interior peace and even spiritual joy.[32]

This is the wisdom of the Cross (1 Cor 1:23–24)—the rich fruit born of James's admonition to "count it all joy, my brethren, when you meet various trials" (Jas 1:2). The Church of the twenty-first century needs to re-appropriate this wisdom. Praise be to God, who gives generously to all who ask (Jas 1:5).

---

32 John Paul II, *Savifici Doloris*, 26.

CHAPTER 5

Sacred Tradition, Source of the Written Gospels

"[Y]ou hold the faith of our Lord Jesus Christ..."
James 2:1

FOR MANY OF THE CHRISTIANS OUTSIDE OF the Catholic and Orthodox Churches, "Tradition" is viewed with deep suspicion, if not condemned outright. Ironically, these Christians do so because they have been educated in a religious *tradition* that limits God's revelation to those elements put down in writing. It is a stance foreign to the Jewish faith from which Christianity sprang, is unsupported in the texts of the New Testament, and fails to recognize Tradition's role in the composition of the four canonical gospels and, as we saw in our first chapter, the formation of the NT canon. The Epistle of James, in its unattributed use of Christ's words, provides a perfect opportunity to explain Sacred Tradition's relationship to Scripture and its necessity if we are to possess the fullness of God's revealed truth.

JAMES'S USE OF CHRIST'S WORDS

Anyone already familiar with the written gospels, especially Matthew's Sermon on the Mount, is sure to recognize Christ's words in the Epistle of James. Two examples tend to jump out at readers:

JAMES	MATTHEW
But above all, my brethren, do not swear either by heaven or by earth or with any other oath, but let your yes be yes and your no be no, that you may not fall under condemnation. (5:12)	Do not swear at all, either by heaven... or by the earth... Let what you say be simply 'Yes' or 'No'; anything more than this comes from the Evil One. (5:34–37)
Your riches have rotted and your garments are moth-eaten. Your gold and silver have rusted and their rust will be evidence against you and will eat your flesh like fire. (5:2–3)	Do not lay up for yourselves treasures on earth, where moth and rust consume and where thieves break in and steal. (6:19)

While not as overt as those above, there are a number of other passages where James's teaching echoes that of Christ's in Matthew's Gospel:

JAMES	MATTHEW
If any of you lacks wisdom, let him ask God, who gives to all men generously... (1:5)	Ask and it will be given to you... (7:7)
But be doers of the word, and not hearers only, deceiving yourselves. (1:22)	Every one then who hears these words of mine and does them will be like a wise man who built his house upon the rock... (7:24)
Has not God chosen those who are poor in the world to be rich in faith and heirs of the kingdom which he has promised to those who love him? (2:5)	Blessed are the poor in spirit, for theirs is the kingdom of heaven. (5:3)
Can a fig tree, my brethren, yield olives, or a grapevine figs? (3:12)	You will know them by their fruits. Are grapes gathered from thorns, or figs from thistles? (7:16)
You do not have, because you do not ask. (4:2)	Ask and it will be given you... (7:7)
Do not speak evil against another, brethren. He that speaks evil against a brother or judges his brother, speaks evil against the law and judges the law. But if you judge the law, you are not a doer of the law but a judge. (4:11)	You have heard that it was said to the men of old, "You shall not kill; and whoever kills shall be liable to judgment." But I say to you that every one who is angry with his brother shall be liable to judgment; whoever insults his brother shall be liable to the council, and whoever says, "You fool!" shall be liable to the hell of fire. (5:21–22)
But who are you that you judge your neighbor? (4:12)	Judge not, that you be not judged. (7:1)

There are also instances where James's formulations of Jesus's sayings more closely resemble those found in Luke than those found in Matthew.

JAMES	LUKE	MATTHEW
For judgment is without mercy to one who has shown no mercy; yet mercy triumphs over judgment. (2:13)	Be merciful, even as your Father is merciful. Judge not, and you will not be judged. (6:36–37)	Blessed are the merciful, for they shall obtain mercy. (5:7) Judge not, that you be not judged. For with the judgment you pronounce you will be judged, and the measure you give will be the measure you get. (7:1–2)
Be wretched and *mourn and weep*. Let your laughter be turned to mourning and your joy to dejection. (4:9)	Woe to you that laugh now, for you shall *mourn and weep*. (6:25)	Blessed are those who mourn… (5:4)
Come now you rich, weep and howl for the miseries that are coming upon you. (5:1)	But woe to you that are rich, for you have received your consolation. Woe to you that are full now, for you shall hunger. (6:24–25)	*No parallel saying*

As I stated in earlier chapters, internal evidence and James's martyrdom in AD 62 point to an early date of composition—the late 40s or early 50s. Scholarship generally assigns the composition of Matthew and Luke to AD 70–90, with Mark slightly earlier.[1] This means that the Epistle of James furnishes us with the earliest *written* record of Jesus's words.

Ironically, if we did not have the texts of Matthew and Luke with which to compare James, we would never know that James had incorporated Jesus's words into his letter. James never identified Jesus as their source! This is curious to us modern readers, but it makes sense once we recall the great authority with which Christ invested the apostles: "He who hears *you* hears *me*" (Lk 10:16).

---

[1] Mark is generally assigned to the late 60s or early 70s. Personally, I think that the lack of comment in Matthew, Mark, and Luke on the fulfillment of Jesus's prophecy about the destruction of Jerusalem is a strong argument for dating all three to the 60s.

When the apostles spoke, it was received by the Church as Christ speaking in and through them. There was no need to stop and identify every time they quoted Jesus's earthly teaching. Through the Spirit, in their preaching and instruction, the apostles handed on the revelation they received from Christ, explaining it with the greater clarity they obtained following his Resurrection, and tailoring it to their respective audiences. This explains the variations we find when Christ's words were committed to writing, as evidenced in the above comparisons between James, Matthew, and Luke.

James penned his epistle at a time when the entire content of the gospel was contained *orally* in the Church's Tradition. Christianity was constituted, not as a religion of the book, but of the *Word made flesh*—alive and active in the ministry of the apostles. Jesus did not record his moral teaching or parables, nor write a monograph about the significance of his death and resurrection. He did not send forth the apostles with a command to write. No, his command was, "Go therefore and make disciples of all nations, *baptizing* them in the name of the Father and of the Son and of the Holy Spirit, *teaching them* to observe *all that I have commanded you*" (Mt 28:18–20).

This totality of life and belief that the apostles communicated to the Church is what we Catholics call Tradition, or Sacred Tradition. It must be distinguished from the pious opinions and customary ways of doing things (referred to generically as *traditions*) that developed over the centuries. Sacred Tradition refers specifically to "what was handed on by the Apostles," and "includes everything which contributes toward the holiness of life and increase in faith of the people of God."[2] The Church hands on this Tradition in its "teaching, life and worship."[3] From this point of view, Scripture can be spoken of as an element of the wider Tradition.

TRADITION IN FIRST-CENTURY JUDAISM & CHRISTIANITY

In the first century, the content of most Jewish people's faith went beyond the *Tanakh*—the *Torah, Nevi'im* (Prophets), and *Ketuvim* (Writings). Tradition was also extremely important. The *Mishnah*, assembled around AD 200, recorded the Jewish belief

---

[2] Second Vatican Council, *Constitution on Divine Revelation*, 7, http://www.vatican.va/archive/hist_councils/ii_vatican_council/documents/vat-ii_const_19651118_dei-verbum_en.html.

[3] Ibid.

that, in addition to the written Torah, there had always existed a complementary oral body of truth, an *oral Torah*. Referring to this oral Torah, the *Mishnah* states, "Moses received the Torah on Sinai, and handed it down to Joshua; Joshua to the Elders; the Elders to the prophets; and the prophets handed it down to the men of the Great Assembly."[4] The oral Torah was regarded as a necessary complement to the written Torah. In the sacred texts, for example, God commanded that various sacrifices be made; but the oral Torah contained the explanation of how priests were to carry them out. By the first century, the authority to elucidate the Torah was believed to have devolved upon the scribes and Pharisees.[5] Jesus, while critical of both groups, certainly seems to have agreed with this assessment of their authority: "The scribes and the Pharisees *sit on Moses's seat*; so practice and observe *whatever they tell you*, but not what they do; for they preach, but do not practice" (Mt 23:2–3).

In the first-century synagogue, it was impossible to fully proclaim scripture apart from oral tradition. Hebrew, you recall, was written without vowels. As in English, there were a number of words that shared the same consonants; and context was not always sufficient to determine an author's meaning. It was *scribal tradition*, passed from one generation to the next, which determined how the text was read to the congregation. Scripture and the interpretive tradition were intertwined. Between the seventh and tenth centuries AD, a group of Jewish scribes, the Masoretes, added vowel points above and below consonants. This determined the "official" text for subsequent generations of Jewish readers.[6]

It is common to hear Jesus characterized as the enemy of Jewish oral tradition, but this is inaccurate. He opposed certain elements of it—such as the Pharisees' and the School of Shammai's strict interpretation of *korban*.[7] Their interpretation had the effect of nullifying the commandment to honor one's father and mother. Jesus taught that, in this instance, the Pharisees' legal opinion was

---

4   Mishnah-tractate *Avot* 1:1, quoted in Abraham Cohen, *Everyman's Talmud: The Major Teachings of the Rabbinic Sages* (New York: Schocken Books, 1995), xxxvi.
5   I. Renov, "The Seat of Moses," *Israel Exploration Journal* 5.4 (1955), 265.
6   Timothy Michael Law, *When God Spoke Greek: The Septuagint and the Making of the Christian Bible* (New York: Oxford University Press, 2013), 23.
7   By vowing that his wealth was *korban*, or "dedicated"—*should it ever be needed*—to the upkeep of the Temple, a man might avoid spending it on morally obligatory things such as providing for his aged parents.

not the doctrine of God (oral Torah) but "the precepts of men" (Mt 15:3–9). Jesus did accept other traditions—such as the one regarding Moses's seat (Mt 23:2) and that the prophet Zechariah had been martyred in the Temple (Mt 23:35).[8]

The apostles also made use of extra-biblical Jewish traditions. Paul recounted the tradition that the rock that gushed water after it was struck by Moses (Ex 17:5–6) followed the Israelites throughout their forty years in the wilderness (1 Cor 10:4).[9] In 2 Timothy 3:8, Paul used the names that Jewish tradition ascribed to the magicians who opposed Moses, Jannes and Jambres. The author of the Epistle to the Hebrews recalled the tradition that Moses received the Law not directly from God, as one would assume from the Book of Exodus, but through the mediation of angels (Heb 2:2). Jude expected his readers to know the story of how Satan and the Archangel Michael argued over the body of Moses (Jude 9).[10] He also quoted the prophecy of Enoch (Jude 14–15).[11]

Jewish oral tradition was alive and well in the Church. That being the case, we should not be surprised that Christ's Jewish apostles communicated the gospel via a Tradition (*paradosis* in Greek) they received from Christ. And so we find St. Paul telling the Corinthians, "I commend you because you remember me in everything and maintain the traditions [*paradoseis*] even as I have delivered them to you," and "I *received* [*paralebon*] from the Lord what I also *delivered* [*paredōka*] to you (1 Cor 11:2, 23; cf. 15:3). Paul ordered the Thessalonians to "stand firm and hold to the traditions [*paradoseis*] which you were taught by us, either *by word of mouth* or by letter" (2 Thess 2:15), and to "keep away from any brother who is living in idleness and not in accord with the tradition [*paradosin*] that you received from us" (2 Thess 3:6).

NOURISHING THE CHURCH WITH THE WORD

The apostles entrusted the Tradition to those whom they ordained to ministry. These men, in turn, entrusted the Tradition

---

[8] This tradition regarding Zechariah's death was later recorded in the *Targum on Lamentations* 2, 20; Scott Hahn and Curtis Mitch, *The Ignatius Study Bible: New Testament* (San Francisco: Ignatius Press, 2010), 49.
[9] Mishnah-tractates *Taanit* 9a and *Bava Metizia* 86b.
[10] Recorded in *The Assumption of Moses*.
[11] Jude quoted from the *Book of Enoch* 1:9.

to others. Paul's pastoral epistles bear witness to the process: Paul instructed Timothy, "what you have heard from me before many witnesses entrust to faithful men who will be able to teach others" (2 Tim 2:2). These were the elders (*presbuteroi*) and bishops (*episkopoi*) we read of in Acts and the epistles (Acts 14:23; 20:28; 1 Pet 5:1–5; 1 Tim 4:14; 5:17). Paul stressed their essential function to his co-worker Titus: "*That is why I left you in Crete*, that you might amend what was defective and *appoint elders in every town* as I directed you... [A] bishop, as God's steward, must be blameless... he must hold fast to the sure word *as taught*, so that he may be able to *give instruction in sound doctrine* and also to confute those who contradict it" (Titus 1:5,7,9).

Just as scribal tradition was necessary for a correct reading of the Hebrew Scriptures, so apostolic Tradition was needed to correctly interpret those same Scriptures. Look carefully at Paul's instruction to Timothy:

> [A]s for you, continue in *what you have learned and have firmly believed* [i.e., the apostolic Tradition], knowing from whom you learned it and how *from childhood you have been acquainted with the Sacred Writings* [the Hebrew Scriptures] which are able to instruct for salvation *through faith in Christ Jesus*. All Scripture is inspired by God and profitable for teaching, for reproof, for correction, and for training in righteousness, that the man of God may be complete, equipped for every good work. (2 Tim 3:14–17)

The apostolic Tradition illuminates the Hebrew Scriptures, showing how they reveal Christ, his new covenant, and the manner of life to which we have been called.[12] God's entrustment of both Tradition

---

12 The apostles learned this exegesis of the OT from Christ himself. Jesus read and explained Isaiah in the synagogue at Nazareth (Lk 4:16–27), revealed the intent of the Law in the Sermon on the Mount (Mt 5–7), debated the meaning of Ps 110 with the Pharisees (Mt 22:41–46), and interpreted "all" of the OT prophecies and foreshadowings of his Paschal Mystery for the disciples at Emmaus and then the Twelve (Lk 24:25–27, 44–47).

We find several examples of such exegesis in Paul: Christ is Abraham's promised "seed" (singular) and the recipient of God's promises (Gal 3:16); Christ is the Church's Passover Lamb, and the Eucharist our Passover feast (1 Cor 5:7–8); Israel's passage through the Red Sea and circumcision prefigured baptism (1 Cor 10:1–7;

and Scripture to the Church render the Church "the pillar and bulwark of the truth" (1 Tim 3:15).

In the first century, Scripture reading was a communal experience. It had to be; literacy rates were abysmal in the ancient world. Scholars estimate that no more than ten percent of a given population could read.[13] Even if we triple that number, seven out of every ten people would have depended upon someone else to read Scripture to them. Combine this with the cost of producing copies of scrolls, and you understand why the only experience of the biblical word for the vast majority of Jews and early Christians was within the synagogue or Eucharistic celebration.[14] That was also where the apostles and elders shared the great Tradition and applied it to the life of the nascent community.

Although preaching was the apostles' primary medium for transmitting the Tradition, they also made use of epistles (thus, the book you are holding). The epistles, by their very nature, were limited in scope — addressing the needs of specific communities or individuals (Philemon, Titus, Timothy). They were far more than mere letters, though. Like the Hebrew Scriptures, the Church recognized these documents as *inspired* [*theopneustos*], literally "God-breathed" (2 Tim 3:16). In the *Constitution on Divine Revelation* (1965), the Church explained inspiration in this manner: "In composing the sacred books, God chose men and while employed by Him they made use of *their powers and abilities*, so that *with Him acting in them and through them*, they, as *true authors*, consigned to writing *everything and only those things* which He wanted."[15] The apostles when writing received the same divine assistance and protection from error that they did in their oral proclamation, and thus their epistles were treasured and shared by those who received them. We find Peter referring to Paul's letters on par with the Hebrew Scriptures (2 Pet 3:15–16). Like the earlier Scriptures, the apostolic epistles were proclaimed orally at the Eucharist, or "New

Col 2:11–12). Paul also taught that the Mosaic tenet "You shall not muzzle an ox when it is treading out the grain" (Deut 25:4) was given to teach that ministers should have their material needs met by the community they served (1 Tim 5:18).
13   Meier, *Marginal Jew* (New York: Doubleday, 1991), 1:274.
14   Notice in the gospels how, when Jesus instructs *the crowds* in Scripture, as opposed to the scribes and Pharisees, he prefaces his remarks, "You have *heard* that it was *said*" (Mt 5:21, 27, 33, 38, 43); Law, *When God Spoke Greek*, 90.
15   Second Vatican Council, *Constitution on Divine Revelation*, 11.

Testament" (Lk 22:20).[16] The Book of Revelation, addressed to the seven churches in Asia, pronounced a blessing upon "he who reads aloud the words of the prophecy, and blessed are those who hear, and who keep what is written therein" (Rev 1:3; cf. Col 4:16).

THE WRITTEN GOSPELS

The written gospels were the end product of a three-step process: 1) Christ's life, teaching, and paschal mystery; 2) the apostolic preaching; and 3) the literary efforts of Matthew, Mark, Luke, and John. We discussed the first two stages above, but I would like to make a point about the apostolic preaching before moving on to the work of the four evangelists.

When the apostles preached, each drew from the Tradition those words and actions of Jesus that best met their individual audiences' needs. Initially, their preaching focused upon Christ's redemptive sacrifice and resurrection. But those required an explanation, and that was found in what preceded it—Christ's life, teaching, and miracles. Each apostle had his own recollections of Jesus and manner of recounting them, his own personality and theological emphases.[17] For confirmation we need only contrast the "literary preaching" that has come down to us in the epistles of James, Peter, and John.

We must keep the apostolic preaching in mind when reading the gospels, since the same principles hold true. Sacred Tradition—the deposit of truth entrusted to the apostles—was the source from which the evangelists drew Christ's words and actions in the construction of their narratives. Luke, who was not an eyewitness to Christ's life, began his gospel by stating, "I myself have *carefully investigated everything* from the beginning...*just as they were handed down* [*paradidomi*] *to us* by those who from the first were *eyewitnesses and servants of the word*" (Lk 1:3,2, NABRE). Even though the four evangelists were inspired, the Spirit did not spare them the effort required of all authors.

Each gospel bears the mark of its human author. "Of the many elements [the four evangelists had] at hand they reported some, summarized others, and developed still others in accordance with

---

16 Over the next century, "New Testament" was extended from the sacrament to the writings proclaimed at its celebration.
17 Augustin Bea, *The Study of the Synoptic Gospels: New Approaches and Outlooks* (New York: Harper & Row, 1965), 37.

the needs of the various churches."[18] This accounts for many of the so-called contradictions between the four gospels. The sequence, for instance, in which the evangelists narrate Christ's life differs in some respects. This is not a challenge to the Catholic's faith in the inerrancy of Scripture. The Church has always understood that the order in which the evangelists recounted Christ's words and actions was not meant as a rigid assertion of chronology. In AD 135, Papias of Hierapolis wrote of Mark's Gospel:

> Mark having become the interpreter of Peter, wrote down accurately whatsoever he remembered. It was not, however, in exact order that he related the sayings or deeds of Christ. For he neither heard the Lord nor accompanied Him. But afterwards, as I said, he accompanied Peter, who accommodated his instructions to the necessities [of his hearers], but with no intention of giving a regular narrative of the Lord's sayings. Wherefore Mark made no mistake in thus writing some things as he remembered them. For of one thing he took especial care, not to omit anything he had heard, and not to put anything fictitious into the statements.[19]

We are used to reading modern historical texts, but the evangelists were inspired to write according to the conventions of *their* time.

The Catholic exegete is also not shocked to discover subtle differences in the wording of Christ's sayings. There were no audio recorders in the first century, and the apostles were not stenographers. When the sacred writers drew from the Tradition, they sometimes communicated the sense of Jesus's words instead of exact quotations. An example from earlier in the chapter:

JAMES 3:12	MATTHEW 7:16	LUKE 6:44
Can a fig tree, my brethren, yield olives, or a grapevine figs?	You will know them by their fruits. Are grapes gathered from thorns, or figs from thistles?	... for each tree is known by its own fruit. For figs are not gathered from thorns, nor are grapes picked from a bramble bush.

---

18 Pontifical Biblical Commission, *The Historicity of the Gospels* (1964), https://www.ewtn.com/catholicism/library/historicity-of-the-gospels-2318.

19 Papias, *Exposition of the Sayings of the Lord*, preserved in Eusebius's *History of the Church*, 3, 39, 15, http://www.earlychristianwritings.com/text/papias.html.

The meaning asserted by each of the inspired authors is the same, even if the phrasing differs. The truth that the author means to assert also explains what might appear as small contradictions. When Jesus, for instance, sends out the Twelve in Matthew 10:9–10, he tells them to take nothing for the journey, "no gold, nor silver, nor copper in your belts, no bag for your journey, nor two tunics, nor sandals, *nor a staff*; for the laborer deserves his food"; and yet in Mark 6:8–11 we read, "[Jesus] charged them to take nothing for their journey *except a staff*; no bread, no bag, no money in their belt." While there are different ways to explain the discrepancy, I suggest that, whether Jesus said to take a staff or not, the memory drawn from the Tradition, and asserted by both authors, was that Christ instructed the Twelve to look to God to supply their material needs. The contradiction is only apparent; both authors assert the same truth.

The sacred authors also sometimes stress different, albeit complementary, strands of the Tradition. Christ's words at the institution of the Eucharist were reported in two different forms — one by Paul (1 Cor 11:23–25) and his traveling companion, Luke (Lk 22:19–20), and the other by Matthew (26:26–28) and Mark (14:22–24).

PAUL/LUKE	MATTHEW/MARK
For I *received* [*paralebon*] from the Lord what I also *delivered* [*paredōka*] to you, that the Lord Jesus on the night when he was betrayed took bread, and when he had given thanks, he broke it and said, "This is my body that is for you. Do this in remembrance of me." In the same way also, the chalice, after supper, saying, "This chalice is the new covenant in my blood. Do this, as often as you drink it, in remembrance of me." (1 Cor 11:23–25)	[A]s they were eating, Jesus took bread, and blessed, and broke it, and gave it to the disciples and said, "Take, eat; this is my body." And he took a chalice, and when he had given thanks he gave it to them, saying, "Drink of it, all of you; for this is my blood of the covenant, which is poured out for many for the forgiveness of sins." (Mt 26:26–28)

There are elements common to the four accounts: the same verbs (took, blessed, broke, gave) used to narrate Jesus's actions; the identification of the broken elements as Christ's body, and the substance in the cup as his blood. While all of the accounts speak of the cup as the *blood of the covenant*, Paul/Luke highlight that it is the blood of the *new* covenant, while Matthew/Mark stress that it is *poured out for the forgiveness of sins.* Paul/Luke include Christ's command that the apostles "Do this... *in remembrance* [*anamnēsin*] of me."[20] Paul/Luke emphasize how the Eucharist unites their congregations to Christ's sacrifice (1 Cor 10:16–18).

The differences in Christ's words between the accounts are not contradictory but complementary. The fullness of Eucharistic theology was accessible to all within the great Tradition — as were the other *"elementary* doctrines of Christ" such as "instructions about baptisms [and] the laying on of hands" (Heb 6:1–2), instructions never put into writing by the apostles or evangelists. "Consequently it is not from Sacred Scripture alone that the Church draws her certainty about everything which has been revealed. Therefore both Sacred Tradition and Sacred Scripture are to be accepted and venerated with the same sense of loyalty and reverence."[21]

THE FULLNESS OF TRUTH

Sacred Scripture is a privileged form in which Revelation is transmitted in the Church, but it is not the totality of Christian Revelation. Scripture is an inspired crystallization of key elements of the Tradition — a divine lexicon, or vocabulary, that God uses to speak directly to the hearts of his children, both in the liturgy and in their private prayer. But just as Scripture's content was drawn from the wider Tradition, so the sacred texts can only be properly understood when read in harmony with that Tradition. "For both of them, flowing from the same divine wellspring, in a certain way merge into a unity and tend toward the same end."[22] Tradition, for example, prevents us from mistaking the brothers and sisters of Christ as children of Mary. It also makes explicit that baptism can be administered to children (implied in Acts 2:38–39; 16:33; and Col 2:11–12), and is valid whether administered via immersion, pouring, or sprinkling, etc.

---

20 Jesus's final Passover meal was celebrated in the liturgical language of Hebrew. In one of the blessings of the meal, the celebrant referred to the Passover as a *zikkaron* — a cultic act that rendered a past event present to participants. When Paul and Luke use the Greek term *anamnēsin*, this is the concept they mean to reference. Jesus instituted the Eucharist as the *zikkaron* of his sacrifice; see Kapler, *Hebrews*, 107–8.
21 Second Vatican Council, *Constitution on Divine Revelation*, 9.
22 Ibid.

In our first chapter we saw how Tradition and apostolic succession were Christ's chosen instruments to define the NT canon. Many Christians do not realize how essential the Church's Tradition was for recognizing the four gospels. Unlike the epistles, the gospels contained no claims to authorship within the texts themselves; in that sense they were anonymous works. The titles affixed to them, *Kata Markon* ("According to Mark"), etc., were not placed there by the authors, but by the Church — based upon the Tradition attached to each from the moment the evangelists first entrusted their manuscripts to the local community.

When the pope and the bishops invoked apostolic authority to formally define the limits of the NT canon, we see that nothing new was introduced into the deposit of faith; rather, they looked into the Tradition, pondered its content, and then explicitly witnessed to the divine inspiration of twenty-seven texts to the exclusion of all others. This is an example of what later theologians call the development of doctrine: that which is first held implicitly is later stated explicitly.

The shepherds were following the pattern established by Peter, Paul, and James at the Council of Jerusalem (Acts 15:6–29). When controversy arose over Paul's missionary success among the Gentiles and his failure to require their observance of the Mosaic Law (e.g., circumcision), a revelation prompted Paul to go up to Jerusalem and submit his teaching to the judgment of those who were apostles before him (Gal 2:2). During his public ministry Jesus never addressed the matter of whether Gentile converts would need to be circumcised and begin living under the Mosaic Law. Jesus had, however, told the apostles: "I have many things yet to say to you, but you cannot bear them now. When the Spirit of truth, comes, he will guide you into all the truth.... and bring to your remembrance all that I have said to you" (Jn 16:12–13; 14:26). Jesus's promise was fulfilled when the apostles and presbyters met in council. Peter recounted how God had sent him to preach to the Gentiles in the home of Cornelius and how, even before he finished his sermon, God poured out the Spirit upon them because of their faith, apart from any consideration of the Law. Paul and Silas recounted the signs and wonders God had worked among the Gentiles. And James, after showing that the conversion of the Gentiles had been prophesied by Amos and Isaiah, expressed his agreement with Peter's judgment that the Gentiles should not be burdened with the Law.[23] By pondering what had already been revealed—the Tradition—the Spirit brought the Church to a *more profound understanding of it*. A proclamation was issued by the apostles and presbyters,[24] making the conclusion they reached a mandatory element of Christian faith from that point forward: "it has seemed good *to the Holy Spirit and to us...*" (Acts 15:28).

This pattern of reflecting upon the Tradition to arrive at a more precise statement of the truth has been repeated throughout the centuries by the apostle's successors in the definitions of ecumenical councils and papal pronouncements. The Arian heresy serves as a case study: Arius, a presbyter in the Church of Alexandria, Egypt, taught that Christ was "God" in only a relative sense. Christ was not consubstantial and co-eternal with the Father. He was, rather, God's first creation, through whom he created all other things. The heresy spread like wildfire. It was attractive, because it appeared to safeguard the truth that God is one, while avoiding the scandal of this transcendent God taking flesh. Its adherents could cite Scripture in support of their position: "[T]he Father is greater than I" (Jn 14:28); "[Christ] is the image of the invisible God, the first-born of all creation" (Col 1:15); "The Lord created me at the beginning of his work, the first of his acts of old" (Prov 8:22). But this was

---

23 James counseled that a few small disciplinary concessions be made to maintain peace between Gentile Christians and their Jewish neighbors (Acts 15:20–21).

24 During the period in which the New Testament documents were written, the terms "presbyter" (*presbuteros*, elder) and "bishop" (*episkopos*, overseer) appear to have been used interchangeably. Here at the council, the apostles demonstrate that these ministers had been given a share in their apostolic authority by issuing a joint declaration. After the death of the apostles, the chief presbyter in each local church was looked to as an overseer, or bishop, in the sense to which we are accustomed—successors to the full authority of the apostles. The letters of Ignatius of Antioch give abundant witness to this in Asia Minor at the turn of the first century, and whenever writings emerge from other areas, this same arrangement is in place. This transition occurred in absolute silence, with ne'er a word of protest. Why? Clement of Rome, writing even earlier than Ignatius in AD 96, provides what I believe to be the explanation: "Our apostles knew from our Lord Jesus Christ that there would be contention over the title of the bishop's office. For this reason, having received perfect foreknowledge, they appointed those mentioned before and afterwards gave the provision that, if they should fall asleep, other approved men would succeed their ministry"; Kenneth J. Howell, *Clement of Rome and the Didache: A New Translation and Theological Commentary* (Zanesville, OH: CHResources, 2012), 117.

not the Tradition of the Church and not the way these passages had been understood in the light of the whole. At the Council of Nicaea, 318 bishops from East and West came together; and, after listening to Arius and his critics, articulated the Catholic faith: "We believe in one God, the Father almighty, maker of all things, visible and invisible. And in one Lord Jesus Christ, the Son of God, the only-begotten generated from the Father, that is from the being *(ousia)* of the Father, God from God, Light from Light, true God from true God, begotten, not made, one in being *(homoousios)* with the Father.... And in the Holy Spirit."[25]

This Nicene Creed did not introduce a new, foreign element into the apostolic faith — nor could it since public revelation ceased with the death of the apostles.[26] The Church's Tradition did "grow," but only in the sense that what was already contained in Tradition *was articulated more precisely* in response to a corruption. The doctrinal expression of Tradition has continued to develop in response to further questions about Christ's human and divine natures, the personhood of the Holy Spirit, the sacrament of matrimony, the Blessed Mother, the limits of papal infallibility, etc.

Heresies are not the only catalyst for development. It also occurs as the Spirit draws out the implications of already-established truths. The Church has always held, for example, that, in the Eucharist, bread is transformed into Christ's body and that his body remains present so long as the accidents (sensible traits) of bread remain. The Church demonstrated her faith in Christ's continuing presence in the Eucharistic elements by bringing Holy Communion to the homes of those too sick to attend Mass.[27] In the thirteenth century, saints such as Francis of Assisi began to ask that Christ's body be reserved in a tabernacle so they could adore the Lord, sacramentally present, outside of the liturgy.[28] That was the beginning of Eucharistic adoration, a now-beloved form of devotion. Even though it had not been practiced in earlier times, adoration did not introduce

---

[25] First General Council of Nicaea, *Symbol of Nicaea*, in J. Neuner and J. Depuis, eds., *The Christian Faith in the Doctrinal Documents of the Catholic Church*, sixth rev. ed. (New York: Alba House, 1996), 6.

[26] *Catechism of the Catholic Church*, 66.

[27] Justin Martyr, *First Apology*, 67 (c. AD 150).

[28] Benedict J. Groeschel and James Monti, *In the Presence of Our Lord: The History, Theology, and Psychology of Eucharistic Devotion* (Huntington, IN: Our Sunday Visitor, 1997), 209–31.

a foreign element into the Church's life. Rather, it was an example of organic growth from an already well-established truth. Over the past two thousand years, the seed of truth that Christ entrusted to the apostles has grown into a vast tree with fruit-laden branches! The Second Vatican Council articulated the reality:

> This tradition, which is from the apostles, makes progress in the Church with the assistance of the Holy Spirit, because there is a growth in the understanding of the realities and the words which have been handed down. This happens through the contemplation and study made by believers, who treasure these things in their hearts (see Luke 2:19, 51), through a penetrating understanding of the spiritual realities which they experience, and through the preaching of those who have received through Episcopal succession the sure gift of truth. For as the centuries succeed one another, the Church constantly moves forward toward the fullness of divine truth until the words of God reach their complete fulfillment in her.[29]

IN SUMMARY

James's early use of Christ's words afforded us the opportunity to explore the Christian faith's absolute reliance upon Tradition. The Tradition entrusted to the apostles was the material element from which the inspired authors drew. It is the larger context in which Scripture must be read. And as the centuries progress, it grows—not in breadth, but depth—as the Spirit continues to unfold the significance of Christ's acts and teaching. In the next chapter we will see how, over the centuries, Christ's commands to "Love your neighbor as yourself," and "Do unto others as you would have them do unto you," grew into the Church's rich body of teaching in the field of social justice.

---

[29] *Constitution on Divine Revelation*, 8, translation corrected.

CHAPTER 6

Social Justice: The Gospel's Economic Demands

> "Come now, you rich...You have lived on the earth in luxury and in pleasure; you have fattened your hearts in a day of slaughter."
>
> James 5:1, 5

THE CATHOLIC CHURCH'S SOCIAL TEACHing is a vast, largely untapped treasure. It encompasses issues of human dignity such as the abolishment of slavery and abortion, immigration, political action, ecology, and economics. Starting from the text of James, we will discover how the revelation of man's dignity—already begun in the Old Testament and reaching its perfection in Christ—has continued to unfurl itself throughout the lifespan of the Church in its social justice teaching, specifically in the area of economic justice. The popes of the last two centuries have taught quite extensively in this area. My hope is to provide a solid introduction to the subject and whet your appetite for further study.

JAMES ON THE FOUNDATION OF HUMAN DIGNITY

We have already seen that one of the central themes of James's epistle is the correspondence between a Christian's profession of faith and his or her actions. And cultic, or ritual, actions are not enough; we must demonstrate our love of God by acts of love for our brothers and sisters. Why? James answers with one of the first verses in the Torah: it is because man and woman "are made in the likeness of God" (Jas 3:9; Gen 1:26). James paraphrases Genesis; the entire verse reads, "Let us make man *in our image, after our likeness*"—a Hebrew idiom for "children" (see Gen 5:3). God created man and woman to be his children, and it invests us with an unmatched, inherent dignity. We are not mere animals. The second creation story in Genesis uses the image of God breathing "the breath of life" into man's nostrils, constituting him as a "living," or spiritual, being (2:7). James would also have been intimately familiar with King David's meditation on the subject:

> When I look at thy heavens, the work of thy fingers, the moon and the stars which thou hast established; what is man that thou art mindful of him, and the son of man that thou dost care for him? *Yet thou hast made him little less than God, and dost crown him with glory and honor.* Thou has given him dominion over the works of thy hands; thou hast put *all things under his feet.* (Ps 8:3–6)

James had even greater reason to stand in awe of man's dignity. He knew that God the Son became one of us, that he died and rose to redeem us and introduce us into *his own relationship with the Father.* And when a man or woman receives the gift of the Holy Spirit in baptism, they become living tabernacles, walking embodiments of the Temple's Holy of Holies. This is what Christ makes possible for every man, every woman, Jew or Gentile, rich or poor, citizen or immigrant, slave or free, sick or imprisoned (Gal 3:28; Mt 25:35–37). Christ's revelation is so revolutionary that millennia have been needed for the Church to grasp some of its implications.

JAMES'S REBUKE OF THE RICH

The latter part of James's epistle contains a stinging criticism of the rich's exploitation of the poor. Earlier in the epistle, James reminded Church leaders that those who "hold the faith of our Lord Jesus Christ" must "show no partiality" toward the rich (2:1). Those who show such favoritism toward wealthy Christians—the example is the rich being given a seat in the assembly while the poor are forced to stand or sit on the floor—have "become judges with evil thoughts" (2:4). Had not Christ demonstrated a "preferential option" for the poor? "Listen, my beloved brethren. Has not God chosen those who are poor in the world to be rich in faith and heirs of the kingdom which he has promised to those who love him?" (2:5; cf. Mt 5:3). Wealth often proved illusory, a distraction from the spiritual poverty from which every man and woman needs rescue.[1] This was not to say that the rich couldn't be

---

[1] "And Jesus said to his disciples, 'Truly, I say to you, it will be hard for a rich man to enter the kingdom of heaven. Again I tell you, it is easier for a camel to go through the eye of a needle than for a rich man to enter the kingdom of God'" (Mt 19:23–24).

saved,[2] but that their salvation requires them to accept the gift of humility and to use their wealth for the sake of the kingdom, for their brothers and sisters, instead of squandering it upon their own passing comforts: "Let the lowly brother boast in his exaltation, and the rich in his humiliation, because like the flower of the grass he will pass away. For the sun rises with its scorching heat and withers the grass; its flower falls, and its beauty perishes. So will the rich man fade away in the midst of his pursuits" (Jas 1:9–11).[3]

In the eyes of God, those with wealth have a moral obligation to assist their less fortunate brothers and sisters. It was this very topic that launched James into his famous section on faith and works:

> What does it profit, my brethren, if a man says he has faith but has not works? Can his faith save him? If a brother or sister is ill-clad and in lack of daily food, and one of you says to them, "Go in peace; be warmed and filled," without giving them the things needed for the body, what does it profit? So faith by itself, if it has no works, is dead. (2:14–17)

This obligation to care for the poor should not have been a new revelation to Jewish Christians; it had already been set forth by Moses. The Law forbade Israelites from harvesting the edges of their fields or picking up whatever crops were dropped in the process of harvesting; those belonged to the poor and the resident alien (Lev 19:10; 23:22). The Law went even further, stipulating that, every seventh year, fields and vineyards had to lay unused so the poor could gather food (Ex 23:10–11).

James and the early Church also knew what Christ had taught concerning the proper use of this world's goods. Jesus told the parable of the rich man who built enormous barns to house his crops and possessions, thinking he would be secure for years to come, only to die unexpectedly and hear the Divine Judge pronounce him a fool (Lk 12:13–21). Drawing upon Sirach 29:10–13, Jesus

---

2 "[The disciples] were greatly astonished, saying, 'Who then can be saved?' But Jesus looked at them and said to them, 'With men this is impossible, but with God all things are possible'" (Mt 19:25–26).

3 For an excellent discussion of the temptations and dangers connected with wealth and the solutions presented by the saints, see Thomas Dubay, S. M., *Happy Are You Poor: The Simple Life and Spiritual Freedom* (San Francisco: Ignatius Press, 2003).

taught that earthly treasure should be spent in aid of neighbor, thus gaining us lasting treasure in heaven (Mt 6:19–20). The Christian does not horde but trusts that the God who clothes the flowers and feeds the birds, will meet our future needs (Mt 6:25–34).

The teaching of Christ and the prophets was what moved James to take the rich to task. Later in the epistle, he prophesied to the merchant class, chiding their shortsightedness:

> Now listen, you who say, "Today or tomorrow we will go to this or that city, spend a year there, carry on business and make money." Why, you do not even know what will happen tomorrow. What is your life? You are a mist that appears for a little while and then vanishes. Instead, you ought to say, "If it is the Lord's will, we will live and do this or that." As it is, you boast in your arrogant schemes. All such boasting is evil. *If anyone, then, knows the good they ought to do and doesn't do it, it is sin for them.* (James 4:13–17, NIV)

The Christian, in contrast, knows that the entire purpose of his life on earth is to take on the image of the Son—to give, in return, all that the Father has given him, even his very lifeblood (Phil 2:3–8; Jn 15:12–14). Almsgiving is one concrete way that the Lord intends for us to do this (Mt 6:3). It is a response to grace, a manifestation of Jesus's own generosity (2 Cor 8:7–9). And as happens any time we cooperate with God's grace, the negative temporal effects that sin has wrought upon our souls are healed (Is 58:6–8; Sir 3:30; Tob 4:7–11; Lk 11:41), and we more resemble the Master.

Those who refuse to love the neighbor in need do so at great peril. James continues, "Come now, you rich, weep and howl for the miseries that are coming upon you. Your riches have rotted and your garments are moth-eaten. Your gold and silver have rusted, and their rust will be evidence against you *and will eat your flesh like fire*" (5:1–3a). He echoes Christ: "Depart from me, you cursed, into the eternal fire prepared for the devil and his angels; for I was hungry and you gave me no food... thirsty and you gave me no drink... naked and you did not clothe me" (Mt 25:41–43).

James saves his strongest rebuke for those who grow rich by "robbing" the poor:

> You have laid up treasure for the last days. Behold, the wages of the laborers who mowed your fields, which you kept back by fraud, cry out; and the cries of the harvesters have reached the ears of the Lord of hosts. You have lived on the earth in luxury and in pleasure; you have fattened your hearts in a day of slaughter. You have condemned, you have killed the righteous man; he does not resist you. (5:3b–6)

James describes a common phenomenon throughout the Roman world of the first century. After the Romans conquered Palestine and installed their puppet Herod, he took control of the land and divided up many of the ancient estates between his family and high-ranking officers.[4] Former owners were reduced to tenant farmers. Small landowners, unable to compete with the output of the large estates, lost their farms and were thrust into the role of day laborers, receiving a pittance. It was a brutal, hand-to-mouth existence; you can imagine the danger posed when a laborer was denied his wage.[5] Almost two centuries before James wrote, the Book of Sirach lamented, "The bread of the needy is the life of the poor; whoever deprives them of it is a man of blood. To take away a neighbor's living is to murder him; to deprive an employee of his wages is to shed blood" (Sir 34:21–22).

Such oppression flew in the face of the Torah and prophets. The earth is the Lord's; he has the right to limit how the land is allotted and developed. Leviticus 19, to which James has already made several allusions, commanded, "You shall not oppress your neighbor or rob him. The wages of a hired servant shall not remain with you all night until the morning" (19:13; also Deut 24:14–15). The land of Israel was allotted to the twelve tribes, and the families within them, by lot. If a man fell into debt and had to sell his farm, his kinsmen were given the opportunity to buy the land—thus keeping it in the family and allowing the poor man to stay on (Lev 25:25). If the land did pass to one outside of the family, it reverted to the original owner or his descendants every fiftieth year, in the Year of Jubilee (Lev 25:8–10, 23, 28). Isaiah prophesied against the land barons who violated this arrangement, "who join house to house,

---

4   Hartin, *James*, 235.
5   Ibid., 237.

who add field to field, until there is no more room" (Is 5:8). The prophet Amos condemned Israel because they "sell the righteous for silver, and the needy for a pair of shoes—they trample the head of the poor into the dust of the earth" (Amos 2:6–8).

When James writes that the cries of the cheated laborers have reached the Lord's ears, he designates such sins as mortal. The same language is used of the sin of Sodom (Gen 18:20, 19:13; Ezek 16:49–50; Jude 1:7), murder (Gen 4:10), and the oppression of widows and orphans (Ex 22:22–25).[6] James draws directly from Deuteronomy 24:14–15, "You shall not oppress a hired servant who is poor and needy... you shall give him his hire on the day he earns it, before the sun goes down... lest he cry against you to the Lord, and it be sin in you." James says that the rich offenders have fattened their hearts for the "day of slaughter," an echo of Jeremiah 12:3 and the prophesied destruction of Jerusalem.[7]

James says that the rich have "condemned" and "killed the righteous man," who "does not resist you" (5:6). It may well be a reference to Jesus's death at the hands of the rich, high-priestly class.[8] James's language is reminiscent of the Book of Wisdom, where the wicked, who gorge themselves on the world's goods, express their desire to "oppress the righteous poor man" (Wis 2:10). They "lie in wait for the righteous man," because he "reproaches us for sins against the law, and accuses us of sins against our training. He professes to have knowledge of God, and calls himself a child of the Lord... he calls the last end of the righteous happy, and boasts that God is his father" (Wis 2:12–13, 16). Then follows a prophetic foreshadowing of Christ's Passion.[9] The wicked say:

---

6 *Catechism of the Catholic Church*, 1867.
7 Although Scripture states that wages should be given on the same day as they were earned, the point is that wages are to be given in a timely manner so that their recipients can afford to buy what they need to live. In ancient times, before banks and refrigerators and supermarkets, it was necessary to buy *each day* the food one needed, so withholding wages even for a day could be a serious problem.
8 N.T. Wright and Phyllis J. Le Peau, *James: 9 Studies for Individuals and Groups* (Downers Grove, IL: InterVarsity Press, 2012), 49–50. This interpretation is, however, a minority one. It was also advanced by Cassiodorus (c. 550), Bede (c. 730), Oecumenius (c. 990), and most recently, A. Feuillet (1964); see Johnson, *James*, 304.
9 This linkage between Christ's coming and judgment upon those who withhold the hired man's wages is also seen in the prophecy of Mal 3:1–5.

Let us see if his words are true, and let us test what will happen at the end of his life; for if the righteous man is God's son, he will help him, and will deliver him from the hand of his adversaries. Let us test him with insult and torture, that we may find out how gentle he is, and make trial of his forbearance. Let us condemn him to a shameful death, for, according to what he says, he will be protected. (Wis 2:17–20)

Like Jesus, James appears to amalgamate the suffering of the poor with the sufferings of Christ (Mt 25:41–43). A sin against the former is a sin against the latter.

THE CHURCH'S UNDERSTANDING DEEPENS

The Fathers and Doctors of the Church continued to meditate upon the Tradition. The fourth century was an especially fruitful period of reflection. Basil the Great counseled the rich, "Tear up the unjust contract, so that sin might also be loosed. Wipe away the debt that bears high rates of interest, so that the earth may bear its usual fruits."[10] He challenged them, "Will your purse not be buried together with you? Is not gold earth? Will it not be interred like worthless clay together with the clay of the body?"[11] Saint John Chrysostom delivered seven sermons on Christ's parable of Lazarus and the rich man (Lk 16:19–31). In the second he famously concluded, "Not to enable the poor to share in our goods is to steal from them and deprive them of life. The goods we possess are not ours but theirs."[12] Saint Ambrose pointed out God's intention for earthly goods, telling his flock, "You are not making a gift of what is yours to the poor man, but you are giving him back what is his. You have been appropriating things that are meant to be for the common use of everyone. The earth belongs to everyone, not to the rich."[13] In the thirteenth century, Thomas

---

10 Basil the Great, *On Social Justice*, trans. C. Paul Schroeder (Crestwood, NY: St. Vladimir's Seminary Press, 2009), 78.
11 Ibid., 79.
12 Quoted in Thomas Storck, *An Economics of Justice & Charity* (Kettering, OH: Angelico Press, 2017), 10.
13 Ambrose, *De Nabute*, quoted in Paul VI, *Populorum Progressio*, 23, http://www.vatican.va/content/paul-vi/en/encyclicals/documents/hf_p-vi_enc_26031967_populorum.html.

Aquinas would employ his keen intellect to further elucidate the thoughts of the Fathers, concluding:

> Two things are competent to man in respect of exterior things. One is the power to procure and dispense them, and in this regard it is lawful for man to possess property... The second thing that is competent to man with regard to external things is their use. In this respect man ought to possess external things, not as his own, but as common, so that, to wit, he is ready to communicate them to others in their need. Hence the Apostle says (1 Timothy 6:17–18): "Charge the rich of this world... to give easily, to communicate to others," etc.[14]

The key insight is that the proper use of this world's goods is a matter of *justice* and *charity*, or *fraternal love*.

The great leap forward in the Church's enunciation of a Christian's duty in this important area of morality came in the nineteenth century, with the publication of Pope Leo XIII's encyclical *Rerum Novarum*. The societal changes set in motion by the Enlightenment came to a head in the French Revolution's persecution of the Church. Although Western nations remained Christian in name, the Church's faith and morality no longer shaped the West as they had in past centuries. New ideologies vied to fill the void: social Darwinism, laissez-faire capitalism, and Marxism.[15] This dechristianization occurred simultaneously with the rise of industrialization, yielding disastrous results. Wealthy capitalists, who owned the means of production, did all they could to limit the civil authority's ability to intervene in their affairs. Unrestricted competition spurred owners to seek the highest rates of production and return possible, and the labor of men, women, and children was a commodity to be exploited. Wages barely staved off starvation and work conditions exposed laborers to injury and death. This resulted in the stratification of society into two classes: a small circle of wealthy owners and a teeming mass of frustrated workers. It was the perfect seedbed for sowing Marx's theory of class warfare. From the midst

---

14 *ST* IIa-IIae, q. 66, art. 2: *Summa Theologica*, vol. III (IIa-IIae QQ. 1–148), trans. Fathers of the English Dominican Province (Allen, TX: Christian Classics, 1981), 1471.
15 Storck, *An Economics of Justice & Charity*, 11.

of destitution, the siren song of Socialism, with its abolition of private property and State-administered production, tickled the ears.

Leo XIII could not remain silent, and so, in 1891, he issued *Rerum Novarum*, or *On the Conditions of Workers*. In it, he called the West back to its Christian moorings. The answer to the conflict between wealthy owners and exploited laborers was not in a surrender of freedom to a Socialist State, but in the *proper* exercise of justice and charity. Leo saw clearly that the answer was not the abolition of private property but allowing workers to obtain property of their own. Wages must "enable [a man to] comfortably support himself, his wife, and his children," and, "by cutting down expenses, to put by some little savings and thus secure a modest source of income" in the form of family land. When circumstances force a man to accept low wages and dangerous working conditions, "he is made the victim of force and injustice,"[16] suffering under "a yoke little better than that of slavery itself."[17]

The role of the State could never be absolute. It was bound to act with strict justice "toward each and every class alike,"[18] keeping in mind that, in practice, this meant that the "public administration must duly and solicitously provide for the welfare and the comfort *of the working classes*; otherwise, that law of justice will be violated which ordains that each man shall have his due."[19] Leo continued, "The foremost duty, therefore, of the rulers of the States should be to make sure that the laws and institutions, the general character and administration of the commonwealth, shall be such as *of themselves* to realize public well-being and private prosperity."[20]

Capital and labor cannot exist one without the other, and thus possess mutual obligations. Capital must not "look upon their work people as their bondsmen," nor "tax his work people beyond their strength, or employ them in work unsuited to their sex and age. [Capital's] great and principal duty is to give everyone what is just."[21] Leo warned them that "to exercise pressure upon the

---

16 Pope Leo XIII, *Rerum Novarum*, 45–46, http://w2.vatican.va/content/leo-xiii/en/encyclicals/documents/hf_l-xiii_enc_15051891_rerum-novarum.html.
17 Ibid., 3.
18 Ibid., 33.
19 Ibid.
20 Ibid., 32.
21 Ibid., 20.

indigent and the destitute... and to gather one's profit out of the need of another, is condemned by all laws, human and divine," calling it "a great crime which cries out to the avenging anger of Heaven."[22] Labor, for its part, had to perform that work that had been "freely and equitably" agreed upon and refrain from destruction and violence in attaining better conditions.[23] Leo advocated bringing Capital and Labor together in bodies resembling the artificers' guilds of the Middle Ages. There the two could collaborate to better working conditions, create "insurance societies," and promote the overall advancement of their business for the benefit of all.[24] In this way, the need for State intervention would be kept to a minimum. Pope Leo saw clearly that the only means for reaching these noble ends was God's grace and the reestablishment of "Christian morals, apart from which all the plans and devices of the wisest will prove of little avail."[25] Apart from God the Creator, there is no objective ground for the claim that man has an inherent dignity and is, therefore, entitled to justice; without God these are no more than imaginary constructs.

Leo's teaching was the fruit of the Tradition entrusted by Christ to the Church. He acted as the wise scribe, trained in the kingdom of heaven, "who brings out of his treasure what is new and what is old" (Mt 13:52). This development of doctrine was an organic growth, triggered by the new climate in which the Church found herself. Leo's call to create conditions such that more families could become property owners grew out of the divine directive for Israel to allot family plots (Num 34:13–29), and his warning to unscrupulous capitalists of the "avenging anger of Heaven" was a reassertion of James 5:4–5. The popes who succeeded Leo continued this process of articulating the Tradition amidst the epochal changes of the twentieth century.

Pius XI exercised his ministry after Russia had fallen to Communism and the National Socialists had come to power in Germany, penning the encyclicals *Quadragesimo Anno* (1931), *Divini Redemptoris* (1937), and *Mit Brennender Sorge* (also 1937) in response. Pius understood that the titans of Western industry would either give

22 Ibid.
23 Ibid.
24 Ibid., 49, 55.
25 Ibid., 62.

workers a more just share of the profits derived from their work, or they would see their businesses confiscated by violence.[26]

> We must strive that at least in the future the abundant fruits of production will accrue equitably to those who are rich and will be distributed in ample sufficiency among the workers — not that they may become remiss in work, for man is born to labor as the bird to fly — but that they may increase their property by thrift....[27]
>
> ...So far as is possible, the work-contract should be somewhat modified by a partnership-contract, as is already being done in various ways and with no small advantage to workers and owners. Workers and other employees thus become sharers in ownership or management or participate in some fashion in the profits received.[28]

Profit sharing — Pius was a man ahead of his time. In a similar way, Pius made the term "social justice," so popular today, a focus of Catholic teaching nearly a century ago:

> Social justice cannot be said to have been satisfied as long as workingmen are denied a salary that will enable them to secure proper sustenance for themselves and for their families; as long as they are denied the opportunity of acquiring a modest fortune; ... as long as they cannot make suitable provision through public or private insurance for old age, for periods of illness and unemployment.[29]

Pius taught that such reforms had to be undertaken judiciously:

> The opportunity to work... depends largely on the wage and salary rate, which can help as long as it is kept within proper limits, but which on the other hand can be an obstacle if it exceeds these limits. For everyone knows that

---

26   Fulton J. Sheen, *Justice & Charity* (Charlotte, NC: The American Chesterton Society, 2016), 61.
27   Pius XI, *Quadragesimo Anno*, 62, http://w2.vatican.va/content/pius-xi/en/encyclicals/documents/hf_p-xi_enc_19310515_quadragesimo-anno.html
28   Ibid., 65.
29   Pius XI, *Divini Redemptoris*, 52, https://w2.vatican.va/content/pius-xi/en/encyclicals/documents/hf_p-xi_enc_19370319_divini-redemptoris.html.

an excessive lowering of wages, or their increase beyond due measure, causes unemployment... [S]ocial justice demands that wages and salaries be so managed... in so far as can be done, as to offer the greatest possible number the opportunity of getting work and obtaining suitable means of livelihood.[30]

Like Leo, Pius extolled the value of self-governing occupational groups, or what we in the U. S. call industry councils.[31] When society looks to the State to police every element of industry, it becomes "overwhelmed and crushed by almost infinite tasks and duties."[32] Pius articulated what has become known as the principle of *subsidiarity*:

> Just as it is gravely wrong to take from individuals what they can accomplish by their own initiative and industry and give it to the community, so also it is an injustice and at the same time a grave evil and disturbance of right order to assign to a greater and higher association what lesser and subordinate organizations can do. For every social activity ought of its very nature to furnish help to the members of the body social, and never destroy and absorb them.[33]

Problems should be solved and policies made, whenever possible, by those most directly involved.

The solution to strife between different economic groups is not Socialism—whose materialistic concept of society is utterly foreign to Christianity—but each Christian, whether capitalist or worker, consistently living his faith in all of his social and political endeavors, and thus reshaping institutions and society.[34] To drive home this point, Pius quotes the Epistle of James four times in quick succession.[35] First, Christians must "be doers of the word, and not hearers only, deceiving yourselves" (Jas 1:22). Next, he gives praise for the spiritual renewal already underway to "God the father of lights," from whom "every good endowment and every perfect

---

30 Pius XI, *Quadragesimo Anno*, 74.
31 Storck, *An Economics of Justice & Charity*, 24.
32 Pius XI, *Quadragessimo Anno*, 78.
33 Ibid., 79.
34 Ibid., 116–20.
35 Ibid., 39, 42, 44, 45.

gift" descends (Jas 1:17). Pius then admonishes the rich to use their resources in acts of love toward the poor, lest they fall under the condemnation pronounced by James, "Come now, you rich, weep and howl for the miseries that are coming upon you. Your riches have rotted and your garments are moth-eaten. Your gold and silver have rusted, and their rust will be evidence against you and will eat your flesh like fire. You have laid up for yourselves wrath against the last days" (Jas 5:1–3). Finally, Pius encourages workers to remember that, despite the materialistic promises of Socialism, *this world* will never be able to satisfy their *deepest* longing: "Be patient, therefore, brethren, until the coming of the Lord. Behold, the farmer waits for the precious fruit of the earth, being patient over it until it receives the early and the late rain. You also be patient. Establish your hearts, for the coming of the Lord is at hand" (Jas 5:7–8).

Saints John XXIII and Paul VI sought to bring the Tradition to bear upon a post-World War II world. The discovery of nuclear energy, new means of communication, faster transportation, and advances in chemistry and automation were transforming the world. John XXIII wrote:

> Probably the most difficult problem today concerns the relationship between political communities that are economically advanced and those in the process of developing. Whereas the standard of living is high in the former, the latter are subject to extreme poverty. The solidarity which binds all men together as members of a common family makes it impossible for wealthy nations to look with indifference upon the hunger, misery, and poverty of other nations whose citizens are unable to enjoy even elementary human rights. The nations of the world are becoming more and more dependent on one another and it will not be possible to preserve a lasting peace so long as glaring economic and social imbalances persist.[36]

Paul VI wanted to see these efforts coordinated, noting how the wealthier nations had a threefold obligation to provide developing

---

36 John XIII, *Mater et Magistra*, 157, http://w2.vatican.va/content/john-xxiii/en/encyclicals/documents/hf_j-xxiii_enc_15051961_mater.html.

nations with aid, the rectification of trade imbalances, and the establishment of a "more humane world community, where all can give and receive, and where the progress of some is not bought at the expense of others. 'If a brother or sister be naked and in want of food,' says St. James, 'and one of you say to them, "Go in peace, be warm and filled," yet you do not give them what is necessary for the body, what does it profit?'"[37] Paul VI went on to address those doing business in still-developing nations to be "initiators of social progress and human betterment," working "to develop skilled workers, to train engineers and other management men, to foster these people's initiative and prepare them for offices of ever greater responsibility. In this way they will prepare these people to take over the burden of management in the near future."[38]

St. John Paul II, in his twenty-seven-year papacy, made his own significant contribution to the Church's social teaching. His encyclicals *Laborem Exercens* (1981), *Sollicitudo Rei Socialis* (1987), and *Centesimus Annus* (1991) addressed a plethora of economic issues. We will touch upon a few. Like his predecessors, John Paul called for a living wage, sufficient to support a family; but he also called upon modern societies to recognize the indispensable work performed by stay-at-home mothers:

> Renumeration can be given either through what is called a *family wage*—that is, a single salary given to the head of the family for his work, sufficient for the needs of the family without the other spouse having to take up gainful employment outside the home—or through *other social measures* such as family allowances or grants to mothers devoting themselves exclusively to their families.
>
> ... Experience confirms that there must be a *social re-evaluation of the mother's role*, of the toil connected with it, and of the need that children have for care, love, and affection in order that they may develop into responsible, morally and religiously mature and psychologically stable persons. It will redound to the credit of society to make it possible for a mother—without inhibiting her freedom, without psychological or practical

---

37 Paul VI, *Populorum Progressio*, 44–45.
38 Ibid., 70.

discrimination, and without penalizing her as compared with other women—to devote themselves to taking care of their children... Having to abandon these tasks in order to take up paid work outside of the home is wrong from the point of view of the good of society and of the family when it contradicts or hinders these primary goals of the mission of a mother.[39]

John Paul II continued to extol the principle of subsidiarity, warning of the abuses, ineffectiveness, and enormous expense of the "Welfare State."[40] He lauded the work of labor unions, calling them a "mouthpiece for the struggle for social justice," while at the same time cautioning against them being co-opted by political parties and their energies diverted.[41] He recognized workers' "right" to strike, teaching that they should not be penalized for doing so, as long as this right was not abused to the detriment of "the common good of society."[42]

The Church's social teaching has continued to develop under the papacies of Pope Benedict XVI and Pope Francis. Both Benedict, in *Caritas in Veritate* (2009), and Francis in *Evangelii Gaudium* (2013) and *Laudato Si'* (2015), address the effects of technological advancements, the universal destination of the earth's goods, and the inordinate consumption of environmental resources by more developed nations. The Epistle of James teaches that the royal law, the law of Christ's for his kingdom is, "You shall love your neighbor as yourself" (2:8); Pope Benedict focused upon this same truth:

> Charity is at the heart of the Church's social doctrine. Every responsibility and every commitment spelt out by that doctrine is derived from charity which, according to the teaching of Jesus, is the synthesis of the entire Law (cf. Mt 22:36–40). It gives real substance to the personal relationship with God and with neighbor. It is the principle not only of micro-relationships (with friends, with family members or within small groups)

---

[39] John Paul II, *Laborem Exercens*, 19, http://w2.vatican.va/content/john-paul-ii/en/encyclicals/documents/hf_jp-ii_enc_14091981_laborem-exercens.html.
[40] Ibid., 48.
[41] Ibid., 20.
[42] Ibid.

but also of macro-relationships (social, economic, and political ones).[43]

When the laity live by this royal law and seek to implement it throughout their personal, economic, and political relationships, we are like the yeast spoken of by Christ, causing whole societies to "rise" (Mt 13:33).

CHRIST, THE WAY

Like Leo XIII and Pius XI, popes of recent memory have been unanimous in their proclamation of Christ and his doctrine as the key to establishing economic justice. John XXIII wrote: "separated from God a man is but a monster, in himself and towards others; for the right ordering of human society presupposes the right ordering of man's conscience with God, who is Himself the source of all justice, truth, and love."[44] "We must reaffirm most strongly that this Catholic social doctrine is an integral part of the Christian conception of life... [I]t should be taught as part of the daily curriculum in Catholic schools of every kind."[45] John Paul II insisted, "there can be *no genuine solution of the 'social question' apart from the Gospel*, and that the 'new things' [i.e., societal and economic changes] can find in the Gospel the context for their correct understanding and the proper moral perspective for judgment on them."[46] The Church's "social doctrine pertains to the Church's evangelizing mission and is an *essential part of the Christian message*, since this doctrine points out the direct consequences of that message in the life of society and situates daily work and struggles for justice in the context of bearing witness to Christ the Saviour."[47]

The seed, deposited by Christ in the heart of the Apostle James, has grown into a great tree, yielding abundant fruit. In this chapter, I have provided a small introduction. I urge you to pull up a chair, sit down at the Church's banquet table, and "taste and see" for yourself (Ps 34:8).

---

43 Benedict XVI, *Caritas in Veritate*, 2, http://w2.vatican.va/content/benedict-xvi/en/encyclicals/documents/hf_ben-xvi_enc_20090629_caritas-in-veritate.html.
44 John XIII, *Mater et Magistra*, 215.
45 Ibid., 222–23.
46 John Paul II, *Centesimus Annus*, 5, http://w2.vatican.va/content/john-paul-ii/en/encyclicals/documents/hf_jp-ii_enc_01051991_centesimus-annus.html.
47 Ibid.

CHAPTER 7

Anointing and Prayer: Healing for Body and Soul

"... and the prayer of faith will save the sick man"
James 5:15

WE HAVE REFLECTED UPON THE MYSTERY of suffering. But what about healing? Christianity embraces both. The written gospels are filled with accounts of Jesus healing the sick: "[H]e went about all of Galilee, teaching in their synagogues and preaching the gospel of the kingdom and healing every disease and every infirmity among the people... they brought him all the sick, those afflicted by various diseases and pains, demoniacs, epileptics, and paralytics and he healed them" (Mt 4:23–24). When Peter was first sent to announce the Gospel to the Gentiles, he told them "how God anointed Jesus of Nazareth with the Holy Spirit and with power; how he went about doing good and healing all that were oppressed by the devil" (Acts 10:38).

Jesus, in his humanity, made present the divine power that heals, that makes man *whole*. He healed through his touch (Mt 8:3; 20:34), through his word (Mt 8:13; 9:6–8), instantaneously as well as in stages (Mk 8:22–26). Jesus sometimes made use of material things in his healing, such as when he made a paste of mud and his own saliva, applied it to the eyes of a blind man, and then told him to wash it off in the pool of Siloam (Jn 9:6–7). He healed a man who was deaf and mute by placing his fingers in the man's ears and then spitting and touching the man's tongue (Mk 7:33–34). When required, Jesus's healings went deeper than the cure of physical ailments to address the spiritual problems at root: forgiving sins (Mk 2:5) and setting people free of demonic oppression that manifested itself in physical paralysis (Lk 13:10–13), seizures (Mk 9:18), and self-destructive behavior (Mk 5:5; Mk 9:22).

We read in the gospels how, when Jesus sent out the Twelve to prepare towns for his arrival, he communicated his authority to them. As a result, they "cast out many demons, and anointed with oil many that were sick and healed them" (Mk 6:13). Christ's power to heal is still present in the Church. It has been *sacramentalized* and entrusted to the Twelve and their successors in the anointing of the sick. Should this surprise us? We have already seen how Christ entrusted the Church with the proclamation of his Gospel, the power to beget children for God in baptism, re-present his sacrifice to the Father in the Eucharist, offer its suffering in union with his, and write and assemble the books of the New Testament. What would keep him from also entrusting her with his healing ministry?

JAMES'S DIRECTIVE TO THE SICK

Serious illness is an acute form of suffering. It is an experience of our finitude, our weakness and helplessness, and ultimately, a reminder that death lies ahead. We have already seen how it can be harnessed as a means to spiritual growth; but it can just as easily lead to self-absorption, anguish, and despair.[1] Cognizant of this, the Apostle James reminded the Church of the special help that was available to them, something in addition to intercessory prayer:

> Is any one among you suffering? Let him pray. Is any cheerful? Let him sing praise. Is any among you sick? *Let him call for the elders of the Church, and let them pray over him, anointing him with oil in the name of the Lord*; and the prayer of faith will save the sick man, and the Lord will raise him up; and if he has committed sins, he will be forgiven. Therefore confess your sins to one another, and pray for one another, that you may be healed. (James 5:13–16)

James outlines a sacred rite, complete with a designated celebrant, specific matter, and form, that communicates supernatural grace to the recipient — or what the Church will later call a sacrament. James's early description of the rite is corroborated by extra-biblical testimony. In 1963, Emmanuele Testa discovered a first-century lamina south of Bethlehem, which spoke of using hyssop to anoint an accident victim with oil and pray "in the

---

[1] *Catechism of the Catholic Church*, 1501.

Name," for bodily and spiritual healing.[2] Let us examine James's description of the sacrament point-by-point, beginning with its intended recipient.

James identifies it as an anointing for the "sick," or *astheneō*. The Greek term means "weak."[3] The remainder of the passage makes clear that James envisions a significant illness: the sick person must *proskalesasthō*, literally "summon," the elders to come and "pray *over* him," presumably because he is bedridden. If the sickness confined a man to his bed, then we can safely conclude that James visualized an illness of some severity.

The sick are to summon the "elders," or *presbyters*. We spoke of these ministers in previous chapters, noting how they appeared alongside the apostles in Jerusalem and participated in critical decisions (see Acts 15:22–29). Because they shepherded the local communities in the absence of the apostles (Acts 20:17–18, 28), their appointment in every church was of the utmost importance (Titus 1:5; Acts 14:23). Today, we call these officeholders priests.[4] In the pages of the NT we also see them referred to as "bishops," or "overseers," *episcopos* in Greek (Phil 1:1; 1 Tim 3:1–7). After the deaths of the apostles, the chief presbyter in each region succeeded to the apostles' authority and became a bishop in the sense with which we are familiar.[5]

The office of presbyter, *zeqenim* in Hebrew, had a pre-history in Judaism. Initially, they were the heads of families, seventy in number, who assisted Moses in governing the people (Ex 24:9–11; Num 11:16–25). Once settled in the Promised Land, elders formed municipal councils. Under the monarchy they regulated the life of their clans in cities and villages, hearing legal cases and rendering judgments (Deut 21:19; 22:15). In the time of the Maccabees, they, along with priests and scribes, made up the *Gerousia*, or Senate,

---

2 Louis P. Rogge, "The Relationship Between the Sacrament of Anointing the Sick and the Charism of Healing Within the Catholic Charismatic Renewal," Doctoral Dissertation, Union Theological Seminary, 1984, pp. 175–76; Anscar J. Chupungco, ed., *Handbook for Liturgical Studies*, vol. IV: *Sacraments and Sacramentals* (Collegeville, MN: The Liturgical Press, 2000), 155–56.
3 Moo, *James*, 236.
4 "Presbyter" was translated into Old English as *prēost*, from which we derive our modern designation, "priest."
5 Please refer to footnote 24 on page 82 for a quotation from Clement of Rome's first-century *Letter to the Corinthians*.

under the guidance of the high priest. Elders also oversaw local villages and synagogues (Lk 7:3).[6]

When Christ appointed seventy disciples to a second tier of ministry, under the Twelve, it recalled the seventy elders who governed under Moses. As with the apostles, Jesus invested the seventy with authority: "He who hears you hears me, and he who rejects you rejects me" (Lk 10:16), and empowered them to "heal the sick" and expel demons (10:9, 17–19). It seems logical to believe that many of the Jerusalem church's "elders" originally belonged to this group of seventy. There are points of contact between the authority and mission of the seventy and the work ascribed by Paul and James to the elders/presbyters.

The Epistle of James specifically recognizes a ministry of healing among the local church's ordained shepherds. By attaching healing to the ordained ministry, instead of only the charismatically gifted, Christ makes his healing power available to all in need of it, throughout the *lifetime* of the Church.

The presbyters "pray over [the sick man], anointing him with *oil* in the name of the Lord" (Jas 5:14). James used the word *elaion*, meaning olive oil, which was readily available throughout the Mediterranean.[7] The act of anointing also had a pre-history in Judaism. Anointing with oil was the means of consecrating priests (Ex 28:41; Lev 16:32), kings (1 Sam 15:1; 16:12), prophets (1 Kings 19:16), and holy objects such as the tabernacle and altar (Ex 40:9–10). People also cosmetically anointed themselves, or guests as a means of honoring them (Ruth 3:3; 2 Sam 12:20; Mt 6:17; Lk 7:38, 46). The dead were also anointed for burial (Mk 14:8; 16:1). Most pertinent to our discussion was oil's medicinal value, witnessed to in Jewish and Greco-Roman sources.[8] Isaiah, for instance, laments how Israel's wounds were "not bound up, or softened with oil" (Is 1:6); and in Jesus's parable of the Good Samaritan, oil and wine were poured into the victim's wounds (Lk 10:34). Just as the waters of baptism bespeak cleansing, and the bread and wine used in the Eucharist, nourishment, so anointing the sick with oil denotes healing.

Unlike other medicinal anointings, however, this one was performed

---

6 Kapler, *Hebrews*, 125–26.
7 Andrew Cuschieri, *Anointing of the Sick: A Theological and Canonical Study* (Lanham, MD: University Press of America, 1993), 89.
8 See Johnson, *James*, 331.

"in the name of the Lord," meaning in the authority of Christ himself. It was the same authority by which the apostles healed the sick (Acts 3:6; 4:10, 30). It also hearkens back to the passage from Mark, where after Jesus granted the Twelve authority, "they cast out many demons, and anointed with oil [*elaion*, olive oil] many that were sick and healed them" (Mk 6:13); although, as we shall see, the anointing described by James is actually *more powerful* in its effects.

The anointing is made in conjunction with "the prayer of faith" (Jas 5:15), in which presbyters confidently petition the Lord for healing. The prayer is made in the absolute conviction that, as Lord of heaven and earth, Jesus can *easily* accomplish anything we ask of him. It surrenders all pain and all anxiety into the Lord's hands, entrusting him to do what only he can. Remember that, without faith, it is impossible to please God (Heb 11:6). It was the prerequisite for healing throughout Jesus's public ministry (Mt 9:22, 28–30; Mk 9:23–25). When faith was absent, such as in Nazareth, healings did not occur (Mt 13:58). Remember the warning James gave in the first verses of the epistle: "[H]e who doubts is like a wave of the sea that is driven and tossed by the wind ... that person must not suppose that a double-minded man, unstable in all his ways, will receive anything from the Lord" (Jas 1:6–8).

The effect of the anointing and prayer is beyond anything possible to the medical field. James says that the sacrament "will save the sick man, and the Lord will *raise him up*; and if he has committed sins, *he will be forgiven*" (Jas 5:15). During Jesus's public ministry, when the apostles anointed with oil and healed, they effected *physical cures*. It pointed ahead to the *sacrament* of anointing, which heals body *and* soul through the infusion of divine grace. That could happen only after Jesus died, rose, and breathed the Holy Spirit upon the Church (cf. Jn 7:39).[9]

The recipient of this sacrament is, after all, an already-baptized Christian, a cell of Christ's mystical body. When the Lord deals with his Church, it is always an action of grace. When Jesus touches the

---

[9] The distinction made between the anointing originally practiced by the apostles (Mk 6:13) and the sacrament of anointing is also applicable to baptism: John and Christ's apostles administered a baptism of repentance to prepare Israel to receive the Gospel (Mk 1:4; Jn 4:1–2; Acts 19:2–6). It was only after Jesus's death and resurrection that baptism became a sacrament, capable of imparting supernatural life; see Rogge, "Relationship Between Sacrament and Charism," 163.

sick, his power goes to the element within them in most need of healing. If there is sin that needs to be forgiven, then it is burned away in the fire of Christ's love. If the soul has been debilitated by chronic illness, then Christ's strength refortifies it. If sickness has led to resentment of God or caused a man to close in upon himself, then Christ makes his presence known and directs the eyes of the heart back to the Father and spiritual siblings. And this grace of healing, if Christ so wills it, flows from the soul to the body, either reinvigorating it to fight and regain health or effecting a miraculous cure.

In terms of the sacrament, healing always begins in the soul and spreads outward. People suffering from depression frequently report physical manifestations such as loss of appetite, chronic pain in the muscles and joints, exhaustion, and fatigue. People struggling with anxiety have reported heart palpitations, shortness of breath, and nausea. That said, consider how guilt—the product of unconfessed sin—can be a root cause of emotional difficulties such as depression and anxiety.[10] As Christians, we understand that sin is the most deadly condition we face, and so we find James urging the Church, "Therefore confess your sins to one another, and pray for one another, that you may be healed" (5:16). Recall, during Jesus's ministry, the paralytic who was lowered through the roof. Our Lord saw his friends' faith and said, "My son, your sins are forgiven" (Mk 2:5). Then, as a proof to those who doubted his power to heal the soul, Jesus healed the man's body. In the anointing of the sick, healing follows this same order.

James states that the sacrament will "raise" [*egerein* in Greek] the sick person up (5:15). The same term occurs in the gospel accounts of Jesus's healing (Mt 9:5–7; Mk 2:9; Mk 10:49; Lk 5:23–24; Jn 5:8) and raising the dead (Mk 5:41; Lk 7:14; Jn 12:1).[11] The term was also likely to evoke thoughts of Jesus's resurrection. Both senses are applicable here.

First, the anointing of the sick can, and *does*, result in physical healing. It occurred in the early Church; and, if you ask a parish priest, you will hear how it still occurs today—more often than

---

10 Allow me to make clear: I am not saying that guilt causes the majority of depressive or anxiety disorders. I only mean to point out that guilt, a spiritual condition, *can* and *does* lead to such difficulties, which can in turn manifest themselves in the body.
11 Johnson, *James*, 333.

imagined.[12] Surgeries go more smoothly, recoveries occur faster, and some recipients, only days after receiving the sacrament, are transported from death's door to full health. We should not be shocked; Christ is a healer, and the sacrament is his "touch"!

This is not to claim that Christ's touch will always result in physical healing. His *grace* is always communicated in the sacrament; but physical healing, *at least for the present*, may not be his will. Jesus obviously did not heal all the sick living in Palestine. John's Gospel reminds us of this when it says that a "multitude" of sick were gathered around the pool of Bethesda; but the Lord chose to heal only one (Jn 5:2–9). And we have already read Paul's account of how he prayed three times that his "thorn in the flesh" would be removed, only to hear the Lord respond, "My grace is sufficient for you, for my power is made perfect in weakness" (2 Cor 12:9).[13]

When physical healing does not occur, the anointing of the sick renews and deepens our baptismal anointing to Christ's priesthood. The sacrament heals us "of the spiritual blindness which prevents us from seeing that it was necessary for the Messiah to suffer ... to be healed, too, of our lack of faith and trust in God's infinite mercy ... [and] of the deep-rooted selfishness which makes us reluctant to accept suffering."[14] It unites us to the Lord's Passion, empowering us to suffer redemptively.

When physical healing does occur, we must remember that it is *only temporary*. All of the sick that our Lord healed, all of the dead that he raised, eventually succumbed to the grave. The *ultimate* effect of the sacrament will be realized in our resurrection from the dead. From this perspective, James's statement that "the prayer of faith will save the sick man, and the Lord will *raise him up*" (5:15), needs no qualification.[15] We see this aspect of the sacrament mysteriously foreshadowed in Christ's own anointing, prior to his own Passion and Resurrection (Mark 14:8).

---

12   Thank you to my parish priest, Fr. Michael Murphy, for personally confirming this to me.
13   Paul's epistles also recount the ongoing stomach problems suffered by Timothy (1 Tim 5:23) and the severe illness that necessitated Trophimus abandoning their apostolic journey (2 Tim 4:20).
14   Jim McManus, *The Healing Power of the Sacraments* (Notre Dame, IN: Ave Maria Press, 1984), 31.
15   Shane Kapler, *Through, With, and In Him: The Prayer Life of Jesus and How to Make It Our Own* (Kettering, OH: Angelico Press, 2014), 99.

ANOINTING AND JAMES 5:14–16 IN THE LIFE OF THE CHURCH

The Church's interpretation of James and early understanding of the sacrament can be glimpsed in the prayers used to bless the oil. Hippolytus of Rome, in his *Apostolic Tradition* (c. 210), recorded the blessing used by the bishops of Rome, "Sanctify this oil, God, as you give holiness to all who are anointed and receive it, as you anointed kings, priests, and prophets, so that it may give strength to all who taste it, and health to all who use it."[16] In the middle of the fourth century, Serapion, the bishop of Thmuis, Egypt, composed a *Sacramentary* containing this prayer of blessing:

> We invoke Thee, who has all power and might, Saviour of all men, Father of our Lord and Saviour Jesus Christ, and we pray Thee to send down from the heavens of Thy Only-begotten a curative power upon this oil, in order that to those who are anointed with these Thy creatures or who receive them, it may become a means of removing "every disease and every sickness" [Mt 9:35], of warding off every demon, of putting to flight every unclean spirit, or keeping at a distance every evil spirit, of banishing all fever, all chill, and all weariness; a means of grace and goodness and the remission of sins; a medicament of life and salvation, unto health and soundness of soul and body and spirit, unto perfect well-being.[17]

Pope Innocent I provides the most important ancient witness to the anointing of the sick. In his *Letter to Decentius* (416), after quoting the text of James 5:14–15, he states, "This must undoubtedly be accepted and understood as referring to the oil of Chrism, prepared by the bishop, which can be used for anointing," later adding that, "it is of the nature of a sacrament."[18] Pope Innocent also wrote of the blessed oil, or chrism, being used by lay people. We recognize such anointings as non-sacramental, since they lack the proper celebrant. We will return to the subject of lay anointing at the end of the chapter.

---

16   Hippolytus of Rome, *Apostolic Tradition*, 5:2, http://www.bombaxo.com/hippolytus.html.
17   Quoted in Logge, "Relationship Between Sacrament and Charism," 197.
18   Neuner and Depuis, *The Christian Faith*, 618.

I must also draw your attention to James 5:14–16's use in relation to the sacrament of confession.[19] In John 20:21–23, we read how Christ gave the apostles the authority to forgive sins; and we also know that the presbyters shared in significant facets of their ministry. Thus, when James shows the presbyters administering a healing anointing with the effect of forgiving sins, paired with the directive, "Therefore, *confess your sins to one another*, and pray for one another, that you may be healed" (5:16), it bears asking whether it is an allusion to a joint celebration of the anointing of the sick and confession. Is James using such a joint celebration to recommend confession and prayers for healing to the larger congregation? We certainly hear echoes of James 5:14–16 in Tertullian's description of confession circa AD 203:

> [It is not] exhibited in the conscience alone, but may likewise be carried out in some (external) act...whereby we confess our sins to the Lord, not indeed as if He were ignorant of them, but inasmuch as by confession satisfaction is settled, of confession repentance is born; by repentance God is appeased. And thus *exomologesis* [Latin, "confession"] is a discipline for man's prostration and humiliation, enjoining...[one] to weep and make outcries unto the Lord your God; to *bow before the feet of the presbyters, and kneel to God's dear ones; to enjoin on all the brethren to be ambassadors to bear his deprecatory supplication (before God)*.[20]

Origen, writing only fifty years after Tertullian, explicitly linked sacramental confession with James 5:

> [T]here is also a seventh [way that sins are remitted], albeit hard and laborious: the remission of sins through penance, when the sinner washes his pillow with tears, when his tears are day and night his nourishment, and when he does not shrink from *declaring his sin to a priest of the Lord* and seeking medicine, after the manner

---

19   Also known as the sacrament of penance and the sacrament of reconciliation.
20   *On Repentance*, 9, in Alexander Roberts, James Donaldson, and A. Cleveland Coxe, eds., *Ante-Nicene Fathers*, vol. 3, trans. S. Thelwall (Buffalo, NY: Christian Literature Publishing Co., 1885), http://www.newadvent.org/fathers/0320.htm.

of him who says, "I said, 'To the Lord I will accuse myself of my iniquity,' and you forgave the disloyalty of my heart [Ps 31:5]." *In this way there is fulfilled that too, which the Apostle James says*: "If, then, there is anyone sick, let him call the presbyters of the Church, and let them impose hands upon him, anointing him with oil in the name of the Lord; and the prayer of faith will save the sick man, and if he be in sins, they shall be forgiven" [James 5:14–15].[21]

The above quotation is also reminiscent of the directive in James 4:8–10: "Cleanse your hands, you sinners, and purify your hearts, you men of double mind. Be wretched and mourn and weep. Let your laughter be turned to mourning and your joy to dejection. Humble yourselves before the Lord and he will exalt you."

Reconciliation *may* have played a role in the anointing of the sick coming to be associated—almost exclusively—with impending death.[22] Some in the early Church—we see this reflected in the *Shepherd of Hermas* (c. 140)—held that reconciliation could be extended only once for the post-baptismal sins of apostasy, murder, and adultery. (If a believer fell into these sins a second time, then he was not reconciled to the Church but left to the mercy of God.[23]) After the initial offense, the sinner confessed his sin and was absolved by the bishop or designated presbyter. He was then required to undertake a prolonged period of public penance. Even after that was completed, and the sinner fully reconciled to the Church, he may still be required to give proof of his repentance by observing lifelong sexual continence, abstaining from certain occupations, etc.[24] Such consequences caused many a backslider to postpone reconciliation until the end of life.

Even when the popes and bishops stressed clemency and attempted to correct the misconception that grave sins could be absolved only once, the deathbed confession continued as a normal

---

21 *Homilies on Leviticus*, 2, 4, in Jurgens, *Faith of the Early Fathers*, 1:207.
22 Bernhard Poschmann, *Penance and the Anointing of the Sick*, trans. Francis Courtney (Eugene, OR: Wipf & Stock, 2018), 245–46.
23 Peter Riga, *Sin and Penance: Insights into the Mystery of Salvation* (Milwaukee: Bruce, 1962), 82.
24 Herbert Vorgrimler, *Sacramental Theology* (Collegeville, MN: The Liturgical Press, 1992), 208.

occurrence. It was a way for people to circumvent penitential discipline. Once the sacrament of reconciliation had been received and the guilt of mortal sin removed, they received the anointing of the sick and Eucharist to complete their spiritual healing prior to facing God in judgment. (If they recovered from the illness, however, the requirement for penitential discipline took effect.) If a person was close to death, *and unable to make a confession*, then his intention to do so, and the healing grace of the anointing of the sick, overcame mortal sin and allowed the recipient to die in God's friendship.

Gradually, anointing came to be thought of almost exclusively as the *sacramentum exeuntium*, or "sacrament of the departing." In the Western Church it became known as extreme unction, the "last anointing." The term originally referred to this being the "last" in the series of anointings received by Christians, following after the anointings received in baptism, confirmation, and holy orders (ordination). Again, however, in the popular mind, the sacrament was called *extreme unction*, because it was usually postponed until death was imminent.

This shift in understanding occurred alongside the elaboration of the sacramental rite. An anointing, in the form of the cross, was made upon various parts of the body, ranging in number from three to twenty. The custom that came to dominance in the Latin Rite was to anoint the five senses and the feet. With each anointing the priest prayed, "Through this holy unction and His own most tender mercy may the Lord pardon thee whatever sins or faults thou hast committed" by sight, hearing, etc. The great Scholastic, St. Thomas Aquinas, explained the practice:

> Now all our knowledge has its origin in the senses. And, since the remedy for sin should be applied where the sin originates in us first, for that reason the places of the five senses are anointed ... the feet are anointed on account of the motive power of which they are the chief instrument ... in some places too the loins are anointed on account of the appetite.[25]

---

25 *ST*, Suppl., q. 32, art. 6: *Summa Theologica*, vol. V (QQ. 74–90, Supplement QQ. 1–99), trans. Fathers of the English Dominican Province (Allen, TX: Christian Classics, 1981), 2665.

For Thomas the principal effect of extreme unction was "the remission of sin, *as to its remnants*, and, consequently, even to its guilt, if it finds it."[26] By the removal of sin's "remnants," he meant a healing of the debilitating spiritual effects sin has upon the mind, depriving man of "perfect vigor for acts of the life of grace or of glory."[27] Thomas also, with his great fidelity to Scripture and Tradition, insisted on bodily healing as an effect of the sacrament, "but only when it is requisite for the spiritual healing; and then it produces it always, provided there be no obstacle on the part of the recipient."[28] More will be said about such obstacles below.

At the Council of Florence, in the hope of bringing about reunion between Rome and the Church of Armenia, Pope Eugene IV and the assembled bishops published a decree (AD 1439) wherein they outlined what was necessary for a correct understanding of the sacraments. Extreme unction was defined as the priest's application of blessed olive oil to the body parts noted by Aquinas. Rather than a sacrament administered only to the dying, the council taught that extreme unction was for "the sick person whose life is *feared for*." It went on to say, "The effect is the healing of the mind and, as far as it is good for the soul, of the body as well. Of this sacrament blessed James the apostles says: 'Is anyone sick among you?'"[29]

During the Reformation the efficacy of extreme unction came under attack. Calvin's critique was virulent: "The third false sacrament is extreme unction.... [It is] playacting, by which, without reason and without benefit, they wish to resemble the apostles.... [T]hese fellows smear with their grease not the sick but the half-dead corpses when they are already drawing their last breath or (as they say), *in extremis*."[30]

The Council of Trent responded in its fourteenth session (AD 1551). It defended the application of the sacrament to the dying, stating that just as Jesus "provided the greatest aids by means of which

---

26 *ST*, Suppl., q. 30, art. 1; ibid., 2660.
27 *ST*, Suppl., q. 29, art. 9: ibid., 2658.
28 *ST*, Suppl., q. 30, art. 2: ibid., 2660–61.
29 Neuner and Depuis, *The Christian Faith*, 623–24.
30 John Calvin, *Institutes of the Christian Religion*, Book 4, chapter 19, nos. 18 and 21; quoted in Andrew Cuschieri, *Anointing of the Sick*, 33.

Christians may during life keep themselves free from every graver spiritual evil, so did He fortify the end of life by the sacrament of extreme unction as with the strongest defense," since, "there is no time when [our adversary] strains more vehemently all the powers of his cunning to ruin us utterly, and if possible to make us even lose faith in the divine mercy, than when he perceives that the end of our life is near."[31] Trent continued, "It is also declared that this anointing is to be applied to the sick."[32] If the sick recover, the sacrament can be repeated if they again fall into danger of death. Trent also took the rare step of infallibly defining the meaning of a passage of Scripture, James 5:13–16:

> This sacred unction of the sick was instituted by Christ our Lord as truly and properly a sacrament of the New Law, alluded to indeed by Mark [6:13] but recommended and announced to the faithful by James the Apostle and brother of the Lord. "Is any man," he says, "sick among you? Let him bring in the priests of the Church and let them pray over him, anointing him with oil in the name of the Lord; and the prayer of faith shall save the sick man, and the Lord shall raise him up; and if he be in sins, they shall be forgiven him." In which words, as the Church has learned from Apostolic tradition received from hand to hand, he teaches the matter, form, proper administration and effect of this salutary sacrament. For the Church has understood that the matter is the oil blessed by the bishop, because the anointing very aptly represents the grace of the Holy Ghost with which the soul of the sick person is invisibly anointed. The form, furthermore, are those words: "By this unction, etc." Moreover, the significance and effect of this sacrament are explained in these words: "And the prayer of faith shall save the sick man, and the Lord shall raise him up, and if he be in sins they shall be forgiven him."[33]

---

31 Council of Trent, Fourteenth Session, *The Doctrine of the Sacrament of Extreme Unction*.
32 Ibid.
33 Ibid.

The Council continued by listing the effects of extreme unction:

> For the thing signified is the grace of the Holy Ghost whose anointing takes away the sins if there be any still to be expiated, and also the remains of sin, and raises up and strengthens the soul of the sick person by exciting in him great confidence in the divine mercy, supported by which the sick one bears more lightly the miseries and pains of his illness and resists more easily the temptations of the devil who lies in wait for his heel [Gen 3:15]; and at times, when expedient for the welfare of the soul, restores bodily health.[34]

Why, after reading such a summary, anyone would put off receiving the sacrament until his or her final moments escapes me. Anyone suffering from life-threatening illness should *covet* such graces; and God is anxious for us to receive them. We need only summon the presbyters.

Be that as it may, the perception of extreme unction as a sacrament reserved for the dying persisted. The Second Vatican Council's *Constitution on the Sacred Liturgy* (1963) attempted to change this once and for all. It stated that the sacrament was "more fittingly called 'the anointing of the sick,'" and declared that, "as soon as any one of the faithful *begins to be in danger of death from sickness or old age*, the fitting time for him to receive this sacrament has certainly *already arrived.*"[35] It stipulated that the number of anointings should be adapted to the occasion and the prayers of the rite revised to correspond to the different conditions of its recipients. It also called for the preparation of a continuous rite, one that would unite reconciliation, the anointing of the sick, and *viaticum* (final Eucharist).[36]

The revisions to the celebration of the sacrament came into effect ten years later, with the publication of Paul VI's apostolic constitution, *Sacram Unctione Infirmorum*. In it, after recounting the effects of the sacrament listed at the Council of Trent, Paul explained, "We thought fit to modify the sacramental formula in such a way that, in view of the words of Saint James, the effects of the sacrament might

---

34 Ibid.
35 Second Vatican Council, *Sacrosanctum Concilium*, 73, http://www.vatican.va/archive/hist_councils/ii_vatican_council/documents/vat-ii_const_19631204_sacrosanctum-concilium_en.html.
36 Ibid., 74–75.

be better expressed."[37] He then invoked his apostolic authority to declare that, henceforth, in the Latin Rite:

> The Sacrament of the Anointing of the Sick is administered to those who are dangerously ill, by anointing them on the forehead and hands with olive oil, or, if opportune, with another vegetable oil, properly blessed and saying only once the following words: "Per istam sanctam Unctionem et suam piissimam misericordiam, adiuvet te Dominus gratia Spiritus Sancti, ut a peccatis liberatum te salvet atque propitius alleviet." [Through this holy anointing and through His most tender mercy, may the Lord come to your aid with the grace of the Holy Spirit, so that, delivered from your sins, He may save you and graciously grant you relief.][38]

Notice how James's promise that the Lord will "forgive," "save the sick man," and raise him up is incorporated into the sacrament's prayer of faith!

The subsequent Rite for the Anointing of the Sick Outside of Mass is, in this author's opinion, a masterwork of sacramental theology.[39] It begins with the sprinkling of holy water, calling to mind our baptism into Christ's death and resurrection, followed by instruction on the sacrament, quoting James 5:14–15. If needed, the sick person receives the sacrament of reconciliation. A liturgy of the word is then celebrated using either Matthew 11:25–30 ("Come to me, all who labor and are heavy laden"); Mark 2:1–12 (Jesus first forgives the sins of the paralyzed man and then commands him to stand up); or Luke 7:18b–23 ("Go and report to John ... The blind recover their sight, cripples walk, lepers are cured, the deaf hear, dead men are raised to life"). The anointing follows: the priest silently lays his hands on the head of the sick person and then anoints his head and hands (or another body part, if the situation dictates). The prayer that follows the anointing is adapted to the recipient:

---

37 Paul VI, *Sacram Unctione Infirmorum*, https://w2.vatican.va/content/paul-vi/en/apost_constitutions/documents/hf_p-vi_apc_19721130_sacram-unctionem.html.
38 Ibid.
39 I say this with no intent to slight, nor even comment upon, the previous rite, which some clergy still use. (I have not made a study of it.) I am simply looking at the new rite on its own terms and expressing my admiration.

a person of advanced age, a child, a young person, someone facing surgery, or the extreme or terminally ill. The Our Father is then prayed, in which all present petition the Father for his will to be done. The rite culminates in the sick person receiving the Lord Jesus in Holy Communion, uniting him to Christ's death, Resurrection, and ascension.[40] The celebration concludes with a final blessing.

The rite allows the sick person to hear Christ's voice in the gospel and be "touched" by the Lord in three sacraments—yet another tremendous fruit produced by the Epistle of James! The severely ill receive the grace they need: either healing of soul, enabling them to more fully unite themselves to Christ's sufferings on behalf of his Church, or the grace to be healed in soul and body so they can accomplish the tasks Christ has for them in the world.

Everyone who receives the sacrament *receives* these graces, but they are not always *realized* in people's lives. We can erect obstacles to God's grace. The two most common are mortal sin and a lack of faith.

Mortal sin, as we stated in our study of justification, is committed when we freely and willfully break one of the precepts of God's eternal law. Mortal sin is a turning away from God, and has the effect of cutting our souls off from the wellspring of supernatural life. Before we can experience spiritual or bodily healing, our relationship with God must first be restored. That entails a decision to break from sin, contrition for having offended God, and the humility to confess such sin in the sacrament of reconciliation. That is the process God established to restore the spiritually dead. Once that is accomplished, we are able to complete our healing through the anointing of the sick. This, at least, is the usual course of events.

A lack of faith is the other common reason one does not experience the healing communicated in the sacrament. This lack of faith can be greater or lesser. A child may have been baptized and reborn into the family of God, but never instructed or led further in the Christian life. Such a person would appear to be at an absolute loss to receive the grace that the sacrament is meant to confer. If this person was offered the sacrament at a Catholic hospital, it would probably be understood as nothing more than an appeal to magic or superstition. Another scenario, all too easy to imagine today, is

---

40 The Church understands that our Lord's risen, Eucharistic flesh is the seed of eternal life, the principle of our own resurrection: "[H]e who eats my flesh and drinks my blood has eternal life, and I will raise him up at the last day" (Jn 6:54).

the cultural Catholic who has been "sacramentalized" — received baptism, confirmation, and the Eucharist—but has never made a sincere, life-orienting decision to think and live in union with Christ Jesus. This person may know the bare-bones of the Creed and the facts of Christ's life, but doesn't really know *him*. There is no daily union with Christ, and his faith is stunted. He comes into contact with Jesus in the sacraments, but his weak faith keeps the grace of healing from being appropriated. We have an image of this in the gospels: a vast crowd was pushing in on Jesus, coming into physical contact with him; but only one woman had enough faith to *truly* "touch" him—just the hem of his garment, actually—and experience his healing power (Lk 8:45–48).

Lack of faith can also be present in a Christian who sincerely seeks to live her life in union with Jesus, who regularly prays and receives the sacraments, and yet fails to believe that our Lord could communicate such incredible graces to *her*. The *Catechism of the Council of Trent* (1597), when answering the question of why so few who received extreme unction experienced bodily healing, was blunt: "And if in our days the sick obtain this effect less frequently, that is to be attributed, not to any defect of the Sacrament, but rather to the weaker faith of the greater part of those who are anointed with the sacred oil, or by whom it is administered."[41]

The good news is that, because the sacraments are the actions of Christ (performed through the Church), his power is *always communicated through them*. The blockage simply needs to be removed for the grace to become effective.

PRAYING WITH THE FAITH OF THE CHURCH

As a good doctor of souls, James transitions from the sacrament of healing, administered by the Church's presbyters, to prayer for healing, practiced by each of the Church's members. You may recall how James, when discussing suffering, encouraged readers to look to the prophets, especially Job, as examples of patient endurance. He does the same here, encouraging those who pray for healing to look to the example of Elijah:

---

[41] Quoted in Dom Wulstan Mork, *Transformed by Grace: Scripture, Sacraments, and the Sonship of Christ* (Cincinnati, OH: Servant Books, 2004), 198. This portion of the Catechism can also be accessed online at: http://www.catholicapologetics.info/thechurch/catechism/Holy7Sacraments-Unction.shtml.

> Therefore confess your sins to one another, and *pray for one another*, that you may be healed. The prayer of a righteous man has great power in its effects. Elijah was a man of like nature with ourselves and he prayed fervently that it might not rain, and for three years and six months it did not rain on the earth. Then he prayed again and the heaven gave rain, and the earth brought forth its fruit. (5:16–18)

James encouraged those who suffered to await the coming of the Lord, using the image of the farmer who waits for "the early and the late rain" to bring forth "the precious fruit of the earth" (5:7). He returns to that imagery here, with the rain and the earth bringing forth its fruit in answer to Elijah's prayer.

The Old Testament was filled with stories of God answering the prayers of "righteous men," but Elijah's life would have spoken to first-century readers in a special way. Elijah functioned as a prophet in the ninth century BC, when the majority of Israelites had turned away from the Lord. Elijah's prophetic correction of King Ahab marked him for death. A parallel could be drawn between those conditions and the ones experienced by James and his readers: the rejection of the Gospel by the majority of Jews and the Jewish leaderships' persecution of the Church.[42]

Elijah was, and is, a tremendous example of the faith that God can do anything we ask of him. The story of Elijah's prayer for drought and then rain is narrated in 1 Kings 17–18. In between those two prayers, we also read that God answered Elijah's prayers to raise a dead child (17:20–23) and send fire from heaven (18:36–39)!

Earlier in his epistle, James paraphrased the Lord Jesus's words on prayer, "You do not have, because you do not ask" (4:2; Mt 7:7). James wanted Elijah's example to embolden his readers to ask for great things. It is always tempting to romanticize the saints of the past, believing that their holiness is far beyond anything we could attain—especially when the saint is someone like Elijah, assumed into heaven in a chariot of fire (2 Kings 2:11). James, however, stressed that Elijah was "a man of like nature with ourselves" (5:17). As zealous and as devoted as Elijah was to the Lord, the prophet

---

42   Scott Hahn and Curtis Mitch, *The Ignatius Catholic Study Bible: New Testament* (San Francisco: Ignatius Press, 2010), 446.

still felt so overwhelmed by persecution that he asked the Lord to end his life (1 Kings 19:3–4). God wasn't dissuaded by Elijah's momentary, albeit deep, dejection; the Lord sent an angel to him with a cake of bread; and that bread strengthened and sustained him for a forty-day trek through the wilderness to the "mountain of God"—a wonderful image of what God does for us in the Eucharist, especially in *viaticum* (1 Kings 19:5–8; Heb. 12:22–24).

Elijah's prayers for the heavens to be shut and then opened were heard, because he was a "righteous man." Elijah was righteous, because had conformed himself to the *divine* will. He prayed for the divine will to be accomplished. Turn to the account in 1 Kings: God sent Elijah to Israel's idolatrous king, Ahab, with the message that no rain would fall for three years (17:1). After three years passed, the Lord sent Elijah back to Ahab with the message that a downpour was in the making. Elijah knew, prophetically, what the Lord intended to do; and yet, it was God's will to forestall the drought, and then withhold the rain, until Elijah prayed "fervently" for it:[43]

> Elijah went up to the top of [Mount] Carmel; and he bowed himself down upon the earth, and put his face between his knees. And he said to his servant, "Go up now, look toward the sea." And he went up and looked, and said, "There is nothing." And he said, "Go again seven times." And at the seventh time he said, "Behold, a little cloud like a man's hand is rising out of the sea." And he said, "Go up, say to Ahab, 'Prepare your chariot and go down, lest the rain stop you.'" And in a little while the heavens grew black with clouds and wind, and there was a great rain. (1 Kings 18:42–45)

Prayer for healing is *fervent*. It is *persevered in* (Lk 11:5–8; 18:1–8; Mt 15:26–28). Such repetition is not a lack of faith, but an expression of it. Praying for healing was not the prerogative of just the apostles. Before his ascension, Jesus said, "[T]hese signs will accompany *those who believe*: in my name ... they will lay their hands on the sick, and they will recover" (Mk 16:18). Christians

---

[43] In Greek, James says that Elijah *prosēuxato proseuchē*, literally "prayed with prayer." Even though he wrote in Greek, James shows his semitic background, where the intensity of an act is indicated by repetition.

can confidently lay hands on the sick and pray for healing, because we know that it is God's will that they be made whole. God will heal them either: a) instantaneously, miraculously; b) by his grace, working in concert with medical treatment or psychological counseling; or c) by infusing them with the grace to persevere in faith, through bodily death, into glory. We can repeatedly pray for healing, convinced that, as the best of fathers, God hears our pleas and, in his infinite love and wisdom, gives us the treatment we need. (Mind you, as with the sacrament of anointing, we must remove any blockages in our ability to receive.)

Christian prayer is powerful, because, ultimately, it is the prayer of *Christ*. "He prays in us and with us."[44] Jesus has united us to himself and lifted us up into his own intercession for the Church. God has dignified us by making us his co-workers in the salvation of the world (1 Cor 3:9). In his providence, he makes the release of certain graces dependent upon the prayers of Christ's body. Our prayers never introduce an idea into the divine mind or change his already perfect will. Rather, they are the *fore-ordained*, proximate cause for God to release certain blessings. In this way, he simultaneously ennobles us as his children and draws the eyes of unbelievers to himself (Acts 4:27–30).

James's encouragement for us to be bold in praying for God's will goes back to Jesus himself. "If you abide in me, and *my words abide in you*, ask whatever you will, and it shall be done for you. By *this* my Father is glorified, *that you bear much fruit*, and so prove to be *my disciples*" (Jn 15:7–8). After James told readers that they did not have because they did not ask, he continued, "You ask and do not receive, because you ask wrongly, to spend it on your passions" (4:3). When we pray for healing, we must sincerely seek *God's will*, not our own.

These truths have been realized and taken into prayer throughout the Church's history. The lives of the saints are filled with accounts of miraculous healings. We obtain new ones every time the Church approves a cause for canonization.

The laity of today are much more comfortable praying with one another for healing. The charismatic renewal has, in large part, been the Lord's tool in bringing this about. Over 160 million Catholics

---

44 *Catechism of the Catholic Church*, 2740.

in 230 countries have been touched by this movement of the Spirit.[45] It is common for charismatic prayer meetings to end with an invitation for any in need of healing to remain afterward to have hands laid upon them and be prayed over. The same occurs after "healing Masses," when small teams of two or three pray with the sick. With the renewal's openness to the charisms of 1 Corinthians 12–14, and the expectation that God will work today as mightily as he did in times past, accounts of physical, psychological, and spiritual healing abound.[46]

And it is not simply the Church on earth that intercedes for God to heal the sick. James's appeal to the example of Elijah calls to mind the prophet's final appearance in Scripture—at Jesus's Transfiguration. In Luke's account of the event, we are told that Jesus was "praying," when Moses and Elijah "appeared in glory" and "talked with him" (Lk 9:29–31). When Jesus prayed to the Father, the communion of saints was present; and the same is true for us. When we draw near, in prayer, to God's throne, we simultaneously draw near to all of the angels and saints in heaven (Heb 12:22–24). Just as Christ "lives to make intercession" for us (Heb 7:25), so, too, do his members in glory (Rev 5:8; 8:3–4). We Christians actually walk through life *surrounded* by a heavenly cloud of witnesses (Heb 12:1). It only makes sense that we would ask them to join us in interceding for healing. After all, the "prayer of a righteous man has great power in its effects" (Jas 5:16); and who is more righteous than those who have cooperated with God's grace and attained final justification? When God heals in response to his saints' prayers, he draws attention to what he accomplished in them during their earthly lives and inspires us to emulate them.

---

45   Alessandra Nucci, "The Charismatic Renewal and the Catholic Church," *The Catholic World Report*, May 18, 2013.
46   See, for example: Bob Schuchts, *Be Healed: A Guide to Encountering the Powerful Love of Jesus in Your Life* (Notre Dame: Ave Maria Press, 2014); Patricia A. Kelly, *His Power is Among Us: The Story of a Healing Ministry* (Santa Barbara: Queenship Publishing, 1994); Robert DeGrandis and Linda Schubert, *Healing Through the Mass* (Totowa, NJ: Resurrection Press, 1992); Briege McKenna and Henry Liberstat, *Miracles Do Happen* (Ann Arbor, MI: Servant Books, 1987); Dennis Linn and Matthew Linn, *Healing Life's Hurts: Healing Memories Through the Five Stages of Forgiveness* (New York: Paulist Press, 1978); Francis MacNutt, *The Power to Heal* (Notre Dame: Ave Maria Press, 1977); Steve Clark, *Baptized in the Spirit and Spiritual Gifts* (Pecos, NM: Dove Publications, 1976).

God not only heals through the prayers of his saints, he even makes use of their relics, their bones and clothing, to galvanize our faith. A woman who, in faith, touched the *fringe of Jesus's garment* was healed (Mt 9:20–22). Scripture says that "God did extraordinary miracles by the hands of Paul, so that handkerchiefs or aprons were carried away from his body to the sick, and diseases left them and the evil spirits came out of them" (Acts 19:11–12). We also read how a corpse touched to the prophet Elisha's bones, leapt to life (2 Kings 13:21). Catholics continue to see miraculous results from this practice of touching the relics of the saints to the sick for whom they pray.[47]

Above, when discussing the anointing of the sick, I noted Pope Innocent's statement that the laity anointed the sick with blessed oil. I said that, since the necessary minister, a presbyter, was absent, it was not the sacrament of anointing. Rather, in those cases, the blessed oil functioned as a *sacramental*. Sacramentals like holy water and blessed oil are "sacred signs which bear a resemblance to the sacraments. They signify effects, especially of a spiritual nature, which are obtained through the intercession of the Church."[48] Sacramentals do not confer grace, as the sacraments do, but "by the Church's prayer, they *prepare us to receive grace and dispose us to cooperate with it.*"[49] To clearly differentiate lay anointings from the sacrament of anointing, the oil of the sick that the bishop blesses for the sacrament is not given to the laity. Instead, they use oil blessed by a priest, often obtained from the shrine of a saint. Lay anointings were practiced throughout the first millennium of the Church and continue today. In 2010, for example, lay brother André Bessette was canonized. When St. André encountered sick visitors to the St. Joseph Oratory (Montreal), he encouraged them to anoint themselves with oil from the lamp burning before the image of St. Joseph. Cures of blindness, diphtheria, infected limbs, and arthritis were obtained.[50]

---

47 See Joan Carroll Cruz, *Relics: What They Are and Why They Matter* (Rockford, IL: TAN Books, 2015).
48 *Catechism of the Catholic Church*, 1667.
49 Ibid., 1670.
50 C. Bernard Ruffin, *The Life of Brother André: The Miracle Worker of St. Joseph* (Huntington, IN: Our Sunday Visitor, 1988), 40–46.

IN SUMMARY

As the mystery of redemptive suffering gives us a small share in Christ's Passion, so the anointing of the sick and intercessory prayer appropriate — in a limited way — the power of His Resurrection. I say "limited" because, however miraculous the bodily and spiritual healing that is communicated, it is only a small taste of the glory and wholeness we will experience in the resurrection.

CONCLUSION

> "My brethren, if any one among you wanders from the truth and some one brings him back, let him know that whoever brings back a sinner from the error of his way will save his soul from death and will cover a multitude of sins."
>
> James 5:19–20

IF I WAS FORCED TO SUMMARIZE THE EPISTLE of James in only one sentence, it would be, "Live each moment in the wisdom of the Cross, because it culminates in the Resurrection." If I was allowed only four words, they would be, "*Live as Christ Jesus.*" That is what it means to be justified. It is, admittedly, not America's "prosperity gospel." No, James is adamant that we must die to ourselves and the world and its values, if we are to live in God's friendship (4:4). The gospel entrusted to the apostles says that Christ empowers us to love the Lord our God, and his will, above all things and our neighbors as ourselves. Our love must be expressed in our flesh and blood. It is not meted out to others based upon their station in life or how they have treated us. We forgive; and we petition the Father to heal, even as we patiently endure all manner of trial. In this way, like Jesus, we constantly look beyond the Cross to the glory yet to be revealed. We live according to the wisdom he displayed upon the Cross. We live it *in Christ*, as members of his mystical body.

This is the fruit we must take from the Epistle of James. This fruit was grown in Jewish soil and was harvested and offered, by the Catholic Church, to the world. Today's world is *starving* for this fruit, and it will not be able to endure without it for much longer. The West has rejected its Judeo-Christian foundation and is collapsing in on itself. Each of us, like James, has our part to play in bringing the "word of truth" (Jas 1:18) to the masses, beginning with those closest to us. Remember, "he who looks into the perfect law, the law of liberty, and *perseveres*, being no hearer that forgets but *a doer that acts*, he shall be blessed in his doing" (Jas. 1:25).

BIBLIOGRAPHY

Althaus, Paul. *The Theology of Martin Luther*. Philadelphia: Fortress Press, 1966.

Anderson, Kelly and Daniel Keating. *Catholic Commentary on Sacred Scripture: James, First, Second, and Third John*. Grand Rapids, MI: Baker Academic, 2017.

Aquilina, Mike. *The Apostles and Their Times*. Manchester, NH: Sophia Institute Press, 2017.

Augustine. *Against the Epistle of Manichæus, Called Fundamental*. http://www.ccel.org/ccel/schaff/npnf104.iv.viii.vi.html.

Basil, *On Social Justice*. Trans. C. Paul Schroeder. Crestwood, NY: St. Vladimir's Seminary Press, 2009.

Bea, Augustin. *The Study of the Synoptic Gospels: New Approaches and Outlooks*. New York: Harper & Row, 1965.

Benedict XVI. *Caritas in Veritate*. http://w2.vatican.va/content/benedict-xvi/en/encyclicals/documents/hf_ben-xvi_enc_20090629_caritas-in-veritate.html.

———. "General Audience of June 8, 2006." http://w2.vatican.va/content/.benedict-xvi/en/audiences/2006/documents/hf_ben-xvi_aud_20060628.html.

Catechism of the Catholic Church. 2nd ed. Vatican City: Libreria Editrice Vaticana, 1997.

Chupungco, Anscar J., ed. *Handbook for Liturgical Studies*. Volume IV: *Sacraments and Sacramentals*. Collegeville, MN: The Liturgical Press, 2000.

Clement of Rome. *Letter to the Corinthians*. http://www.ewtn.com/library/patristc/anf1-1.htm.

Cohen, Abraham. *Everyman's Talmud: The Major Teachings of the Rabbinic Sages*. New York: Schocken Books, 1995.

Cuschieri, Andrew. *Anointing of the Sick: A Theological and Canonical Study*. Lanham, MD: University Press of America, 1993.

De Vaux, Roland. *Ancient Israel: Its Life and Institutions*. New York: McGraw-Hill Book Company, Inc., 1961.

Encyclopaedia Judaica. Jerusalem: Keter Publishing House, 1972.

Eusebius. *Ecclesiastical History*. http://www.newadvent.org/fathers/250102.htm.

Farmer, William R. and Denis M. Farkasfalvy. *The Formation of the New Testament Canon: An Ecumenical Approach*. New York: Paulist Press, 1983.

Gambero, Luigi. *Mary and the Fathers of the Church: The Blessed Virgin Mary in Patristic Thought*. San Francisco: Ignatius Press, 1999.

George, Timothy. "A Right Strawy Epistle: Reformation Perspectives on James." *The Southern Baptist Journal of Theology* 4/3, Fall 2000.

Groeschel, Benedict J. and James Monti. *In the Presence of Our Lord: The History, Theology, and Psychology of Eucharistic Devotion*. Huntington, IN: Our Sunday Visitor, 1997.

Hahn, Scott. *Consuming the Word: The New Testament and the Eucharist in the Early Church*. New York: Image, 2013.

———. *Hail Holy Queen: The Mother of God in the Word of God*. San Francisco: Doubleday, 2001.

———. *Joy to the World*. New York: Image, 2014.

———. *Romans*. Catholic Commentary on Sacred Scripture. Grand Rapids, MI: Baker Academic, 2017.

Hahn, Scott and Curtis Mitch. *The Ignatius Catholic Study Bible: New Testament*. San Francisco: Ignatius Press, 2010.

Hartin, Patrick J. *James*. Sacra Pagina Series. Collegeville, MN: Liturgical Press, 2009.

Hertz, J. H., ed. *The Pentateuch and Haftorahs: Hebrew Text and Commentary*, Second Edition. London: Soncino Press, 1960.

Hippolytus of Rome. *Apostolic Tradition*. http://www.bombaxo.com/hippolytus.html.

Howell, Kenneth J. *Ignatius of Antioch and Polycarp of Smyrna: A New Translation and Theological Commentary*. Zanesville, OH: CHResources, 2009.

———. *Clement of Rome and the Didache: A New Translation and Theological Commentary*. Zanesville, OH: CHResources, 2012.

John XIII. *Mater et Magistra*. http://w2.vatican.va/content/john-xxiii/en/encyclicals/documents/hf_j-xxiii_enc_15051961_mater.html.

Johnson, Luke Timothy. *Brother of Jesus, Friend of God: Studies in the Letter of James*. Grand Rapids, MI: William B. Eerdmans, 2004.

———. *The Letter of James: A New Translation with Introduction and Commentary*. New Haven, CT: Yale University Press, 1995.

John Paul II. *Centesimus Annus*. http://w2.vatican.va/content/john-paul-ii/en/encyclicals/documents/hf_jp-ii_enc_01051991_centesimus-annus.html.

———. *Laborem Exercens*. http://w2.vatican.va/content/john-paul-ii/en/encyclicals/documents/hf_jp-ii_enc_14091981_laborem-exercens.html.

———. *Salvifici Doloris*. https://w2.vatican.va/content/john-paul-ii/en/apost_letters/1984/documents/hf_jp-ii_apl_11021984_salvifici-doloris.html.

Jurgens, William A. *The Faith of the Early Fathers*. Volume 1. Collegeville, MN: The Liturgical Press, 1970.

Kapler, Shane. *The Epistle to the Hebrews and the Seven Core Beliefs of Catholics*. Kettering, OH: Angelico Press, 2016.

———. *The God Who is Love: Explaining Christianity From Its Center.* St. Louis: Out of the Box, 2009.

———. *Through, With, and In Him: The Prayer Life of Jesus and How to Make It Our Own.* Kettering, OH: Angelico Press, 2014.

Keating, Karl. *Catholicism and Fundamentalism.* San Francisco: Ignatius Press, 1988.

Law, Timothy Michael. *When God Spoke Greek: The Septuagint and the Making of the Christian Bible.* New York: Oxford University Press, 2013.

Lefebure, Leo D. "The Understanding of Suffering in the Early Church." *CLARITAS Journal of Dialogue and Culture,* 4/2, October 2015, 33.

Leo XIII. *Rerum Novarum.* http://w2.vatican.va/content/leo-xiii/en/encyclicals/documents/hf_l-xiii_enc_15051891_rerum-novarum.html.

Levine, Amy-Jill and Marc Zvi Brettler, eds. *The Jewish Annotated New Testament.* New York: Oxford University Press, 2011.

Luther, Martin. *Luther's Works,* Volume 35. St. Louis: Concordia, 1963.

McDonald, Lee Martin and James A. Sanders, eds. *The Canon Debate.* Peabody, MA: Hendrickson Publishers, Inc., 2002.

McManus, Jim. *The Healing Power of the Sacraments.* Notre Dame: Ave Maria Press, 1984.

Meier, John P. *A Marginal Jew: Rethinking the Historical Jesus.* Volume 1. New York: Doubleday, 1991.

Moo, Douglas J. *The Letter of James.* Grand Rapids, MI: William B. Eerdmans Publishing Company, 2000.

Mork, Wulstan. *Transformed by Grace: Scripture, Sacraments, and the Sonship of Christ.* Cincinnati, OH: Servant Books, 2004.

Neuner, J. and J. Depuis, eds. *The Christian Faith in the Doctrinal Documents of the Catholic Church,* Sixth Edition. New York: Alba House, 1996.

Nucci, Alessandra. "The Charismatic Renewal and the Catholic Church." *The Catholic World Report,* May 18, 2013.

Origen. *Homilies on Joshua.* Translated by Barbara J. Bruce. Washington, DC: The Catholic University of America Press, 2002.

Pimentel, Stephen. *Witnesses of the Messiah: On Acts of the Apostles 1–15.* Steubenville, OH: Emmaus Road Publishing, 2002.

Pitre, Brant. *Jesus and the Jewish Roots of Mary.* New York: Image, 2018.

Pius XI. *Divini Redemptoris.* https://w2.vatican.va/content/pius-xi/en/encyclicals/documents/hf_p-xi_enc_19370319_divini-redemptoris.html.

———. *Quadragesimo Anno.* http://w2.vatican.va/content/pius-xi/en/encyclicals/documents/hf_p-xi_enc_19310515_quadragesimo-anno.html.

Pontifical Biblical Commission. *The Historicity of the Gospels,* 1964. http://www.ewtn.com/library/curia/pbcgospl.htm.

Poschmann, Bernhard. *Penance and the Anointing of the Sick.* Translated by Francis Courtney. Eugene, Oregon: Wipf & Stock, 2018.

Quasten, Johannes, ed. *The Didache: The Epistle of Barnabus, the Epistles and the Martyrdom of St. Polycarp, the Fragments of Papias, the Epistle to Diognetus.* Ancient Christian Writers. Translated by James A. Kleist. New York: Paulist Press, 1948.

Renov, I. "The Seat of Moses." *Israel Exploration Journal* 5, no. 4, 1955, 262–67.

Reynolds, Brian K. *Gateway to Heaven: Marian Doctrine and Devotion, Image and Typology in the Patristic and Medieval Periods.* Hyde Park, NY: New City Press, 2012.

Riga, Peter. *Sin and Penance: Insights Into the Mystery of Salvation.* Milwaukee: Bruce Publishing Co., 1962.

Roberts, Alexander, James Donaldson, and A. Cleveland Coxe, eds. *Ante-Nicene Fathers,* Vol. 3. Translated by S. Thelwall. Buffalo, NY: Christian Literature Publishing Co. http://www.newadvent.org/fathers/0320.htm.

Rogge, Louis P. "The Relationship Between the Sacrament of Anointing the Sick and the Charism of Healing Within the Catholic Charismatic Renewal." Doctoral Dissertation, Union Theological Seminary, 1984.

Ruffin, C. Bernard. *The Life of Brother André: The Miracle Worker of St. Joseph.* Huntington, IN: Our Sunday Visitor, 1988.

Shanks, Herschel and Ben Witherington III. *The Brother of Jesus.* San Francisco: Harper Collins, 2003.

Sheen, Fulton J. *Justice & Charity.* Charlotte, NC: The American Chesterton Society, 2016.

Souter, Alexander. *The Text and Canon of the New Testament.* New York: Charles Scribner's Sons, 1913.

Saward, John. *Cradle of Redeeming Love: The Theology of the Christmas Mystery.* San Francisco: Ignatius Press, 2002.

Storck, Thomas. *An Economics of Justice & Charity.* Kettering, OH: Angelico Press, 2017.

Thomas Aquinas, *Summa Theologica,* volumes 1–5. Translated by Fathers of the English Dominican Province. Allen, TX: Christian Classics, 1981.

Thomas à Kempis. *The Imitation of Christ.* Translated by Ronald Knox and Michael Oakley. San Francisco: Ignatius Press, 2005.

Vorgrimler, Herbert. *Sacramental Theology.* Collegeville, MN: The Liturgical Press, 1992.

West, Christopher. *Good News About Sex and Marriage.* Ann Arbor, MI: Servant Publications, 2000.

Wright, N. T. and Phyllis J. Le Peau. *James: 9 Studies for Individuals and Groups.* Downers Grove, IL: InterVarsity Press, 2012.

Van Zeller, Hubert. *The Mystery of Suffering.* Notre Dame: Christian Classics, 2015.

ABOUT THE AUTHOR

For the past 30 years Shane Kapler has been involved in evangelism and catechesis within the Archdiocese of St. Louis. His previously published works include *The Epistle of the Hebrews and the Seven Core Beliefs of Catholics*, *Marrying the Rosary to the Divine Mercy Chaplet*, and *Through, With, and In Him*.

Printed in Great Britain
by Amazon